ISBN 978-1-334-27902-7
PIBN 10570645

This book is a reproduction of an important historical work. Forgotten Books uses state-of-the-art technology to digitally reconstruct the work, preserving the original format whilst repairing imperfections present in the aged copy. In rare cases, an imperfection in the original, such as a blemish or missing page, may be replicated in our edition. We do, however, repair the vast majority of imperfections successfully; any imperfections that remain are intentionally left to preserve the state of such historical works.

For support please visit www.forgottenbooks.com

THE
HERB-GARDEN

By

FRANCES A. BARDSWELL

AUTHOR OF 'THE BOOK OF TOWN & WINDOW GARDENING,' 'NOTES
FROM NATURE'S GARDEN,' 'SEA-COAST GARDENS AND GARDENING'

WITH SIXTEEN ILLUSTRATIONS IN
COLOUR DRAWN FROM NATURE BY
THE HON. FLORENCE AMHERST
AND ISABELLE FORREST

LONDON
ADAM & CHARLES BLACK
1911

'It is a commodious and a pleasaunt thyng to a mansion to have an orcherde of sundry fruites ; but it is more commodious to have a fayre garden repleted with herbs of aromatyck and redolent savours.'

ANDREW BORDE.

TO

MARGARET, LADY AMHERST OF HACKNEY

Contents

vii

List of Illustrations

THE HERB REPRESENTED ON THE COVER DESIGN IS
CORIANDER IN FLOWER.

INTRODUCTORY

CHAPTER I

' Behold, I have given you every herb bearing seed, which is upon the face of all the earth ; . . . to you it shall be for meat.'

PERHAPS it is because I have already written one or two short papers about Herbs that I am often asked to write a book about them. There is not much modern literature upon the subject, a proof of which is that a slight paper of mine on ' The Herb-Border ' was resuscitated after seven years and republished in *The Garden*. This little paper, I found, was being cut out by sundry amateur gardeners who wanted to start a Herb-border or Herb-garden for themselves.

A book on the Herb-garden is wanted, I think, but it need not be a tediously long one. Herbs are the least exacting of plants, and their culture is simple. Moreover, compared with many of our other favourites, such as Roses, Alpines, and

3

Orchids, the varieties are few, and make less demands upon our memories.

How, then, it may be asked, does it come about that books written by the old Herbalists have catalogues of such great length—long enough to fill pages upon pages ? This question is easily answered. The old list included a large class of Herbs of a kind which I do not fancy many people would care to encourage in their gardens, much less to cherish in their sunniest quarters ; on the contrary, they generally cast them out with contumely. Yet they are of great interest to the Herbalists, and swell their lists to overflowing. Cat's-Tails, Shepherd's-Purse (troublesome, encroaching little weed that, but it contains a tannate and arrests bleeding), Dandelions, Daisies, Nettles, Plaintains, were all treasures in the eyes of Gerarde and Culpepper. There is a lively Sow-Thistle who often stares at me from a back border of my Herb-garden. ' My milky juice,' he says, ' is a fine face-wash, and my leaves, if eaten, will cure hares, even March hares, of madness.' But do I let him stay where he is ? No ; I am ashamed to say I root him out, and so, I suppose, would most people.

To make a long story short, there is a large number of Herbs which are most interesting to hear about and study, but few would care to grow them in their gardens. Once we exclude the wildings, it is surprising how the long lists dwindle down. I do allow some of them a footing, and shall have more to say about them by-and-by. In the meantime, plenty of Herbs remain that are both good-looking, uncommon, and useful. Their cultivation offers a wide field of interest and pleasure ; richly do they deserve the comfort and the compliment of a place to themselves.

Modern book-making about Herbs has often consisted in diving into the past and culling quaint recipes and verses and sayings from the old poets and Herbalists. Enough of these can easily be found to fill several large volumes.

There is a great charm about this sort of thing, but I do not think it is exactly what is wanted at the present time. Moreover, it has been done already. In Lady Rosalind Northcote's interesting study, *The Book of Herbs*, the best old writers have been quoted from, and the use of Herbs in magic, in perfume, and in old-time decoration, heraldry, and ornament, been fully gone into. Dr. Fernic, in his *Herbal Simples*, has given to the healing use of Herbs the most complete and ample consideration, making his readers see, I think, that they might do worse occasionally than go back to the use of some of the old herbal simples whose virtue he makes so clear.

What, then, remains for another writer to do? To tell one's readers as simply as possible the way to start and cultivate a Herb-garden, to call to memory the half-forgotten uses of many Herbs, to express the pleasure such a garden may give, and to set forth the difficulties (if any) that beset the collector of Herbs. This is what I should like to do.

Many people who love gardens and gardening very dearly have said to me: 'I would never care for a Herb-garden: you cannot make it pretty.' Well, perhaps I can make the people who say this find that they are mistaken. Others have remarked: 'We like Herbs very much, and would love to grow them, but have no room.' To these I would reply: 'Even a small patch is better than none.' Cooks and housekeepers, again, sometimes say they need not depend upon the gardener for Herbs they want, but can buy them very easily from the grocer in bottles. Bottles, indeed! How much I dislike the sight of those bottles! Cooks who talk like this do not know the difference between Herbs bought in bottles and the Herbs they might gather for themselves on sunny mornings in the summer out of their own or their masters' gardens. If the chance is given her, the Queen of the Kitchen soon discovers the secret !

Since I have started a Herb-garden of any pretension (not much pretension, either), it is amusing to see the zest with which the cook or cooks will go out into the sweet fragrant garden while the Herbs are at their best, and wander around it, gathering a sprig here, a spray there, and a leaf somewhere else, to bring into the kitchen and put into the soups or salads, according to the needs of the day. Never do white soups, julienne soups, potato soup, and many other soups and sauces, taste so good as when freshly-gathered Herbs are put into them. Bits of Thyme, sprigs of Chervil, Borage, Burnet, Summer Savory, Sweet Basil, Sweet Marjoram—all these Herbs have flavours almost forgotten in England, yet our grandfathers —at all events, our great-grandfathers and great-grandmothers—knew all about them, and appreciated them so much that they would amuse themselves on summer evenings by gathering and mixing just the right blends to flavour certain dishes. This mixing of flavours was very important sometimes, particularly so when the season for gathering and drying Herbs came round. Some Herbs—most of them, in fact—would be put away, each sort separate ; but in other cases mixtures or blends of them were found useful.

Things are very different in France. There we find twenty different Herb flavours to one or two that we get in England. Medicinally, as well as in cookery, Herbs are far more used on the Continent than with us. While travelling about in foreign hotels, what weird smells reach us from the bedrooms or sitting-rooms of Aniseed, Clove, Coriander, and other aromatic things ! It was at an hotel in the South of France, quite lately, that I saw Camomile-tea for the first time since I was a little girl in the nursery. It was brought in every evening, after dinner, by a lady to her husband, a famous doctor, then an invalid. The *tisane* looked tempting enough, in a large flat-shaped wineglass, sprinkled over at the top with the small white flowers. Great faith was placed in the old-fashioned remedy.

The French are very clever in the use of herbs for soups—not only in flavouring them (we can do that ourselves), but they can make quite good soup of little else. I have the good-fortune to be acquainted with a French family long domiciled in

England. Sometimes they send me a dainty basket filled with packets or bunches of different Herbs, all ready for use, to make a certain kind of soup. There are *Ciboule, Cerfeuil, Oseille,* and a tiny bunch of Parsley and Mint. These, with a little milk, a morsel of butter, a pinch or two of salt and pepper, and a thin slice of bread to each person, make a *potage* fit for a Prince.

It is rather amusing that of late years the best Herb-borders I have met with in England have been in the kitchen-gardens of people who keep a *chef.* This personage simply will have certain Herbs when he wants them for his cooking. Though not grown in any way for ornament, many of these unpretending Herb-borders look quite fascinating ; bees and butterflies hover over them, and spicy fragrances are wafted from them that remind one of the Maritime Alps.

Now a word about our pictures. It will be seen that they are not all done after one style. We could not very well help this, for the plants had to have their likenesses taken just at the moment when they were ready for it. It was necessary to paint them on the spot, and the same artist was not always forthcoming. In some cases the flower

and seed are shown ; in others, merely the foliage
—for often with herbs the leaf is the part that
matters, and the flower is inconspicuous and com-
paratively unimportant.

THE MAKING OF THE HERB-GARDEN

CHAPTER II

THE MAKING OF THE HERB-GARDEN

'To flower and plant and tree, the garden is a cloistered refuge from the battle of life.'

THE one thing most needful for the Herb-garden is sunshine. Without it there will be neither virtue nor fragrance ; the plants will exist, but will neither be happy themselves nor make us so.

Any good garden soil suffices to satisfy most Herbs, but the same soil will not suit all equally well. Some are naturally rock or mountain plants, and do not mind how dry the ground is. Others, like the family of Mints, love moist places ; one or two, like Rue and Fennel, absolutely thrive in poor soil, while others demand good living. No doubt the old superstition that plants are apt to quarrel among themselves, and that some are absolutely antipathetic to others, originated in the first instance in the fact that there are great differ-

13

ences of opinion among them as to the soil in which they like to live. Rue will not grow near Basil, it was believed, but Rue and the Fig-tree are in league. Dill, Coriander, Mallows, and Chervil love to be 'set or sowne' together, while Radish and Hyssop are at enmity, and refuse to have anything to do with each other.

Yet sometimes in a small garden, in spite of the likes and dislikes of the plants, we are obliged, for want of space, to ask the different families to dwell side by side. It is wonderful how a little management gets over difficulties. The Mints can be well nourished at the roots, and so kept in a good temper, and the lovers of rocky places can be given nooks and corners amid edgings of stone along the borders. Thus all are satisfied. As a rule, Herbs demand a somewhat dry soil and perfect drainage.

Whether we prepare and plant our garden in spring or autumn depends on circumstances. If roughish ground is taken for the purpose, a good deal has to be done, and autumn is the best time to begin. Our site selected, the ground may be cleared, dug over, and the beds for the sowing of spring annuals prepared. Even when the ground is already fit for use, the question whether to plant perennials in spring or autumn is always difficult.

If only we knew beforehand what sort of a winter to expect, how much easier gardening would be ! When the winter and the early months of the year are kind, we are glad to have planted in autumn ; it is pleasant to see the plants spring up already at home. At other times we are made to wish that we had waited till the spring. If we do plant in autumn it should be early in the autumn, so as to give the plants a chance to establish themselves before the onset of winter.

As to aspect, it does not matter what that is exactly, so long as there is enough sunshine. South-east or south-west are both excellent aspects. The site must be absolutely clear of trees, but the shelter of a wall, or hedge, or bank is good.

Our own Herb-garden looks mainly to the south-west. The most southerly and hottest border is filled with Marjoram and several sorts of Thyme, that creep and spread among the stones along the edges. A bank with a hedge on the top of it protects the enclosure all the way round, and protection is needed, for behind it comes a field, and then the wild North Sea. Certainly Herbs like plenty of air, and air in movement ; they drink it in as if with joy, and breathe it out again in fragrance.

Very often a piece of kitchen-garden is portioned off to make the Herb-garden. If possible, this plot should come between the flower and kitchen gardens, where it will be a sort of debatable land between the purely useful and the purely ornamental. The sunniness of it would suggest a sundial, and it would be delightful if the Mints could be given a rill of running water. We could then grow Cresses as well as Mints. At the foot of the sundial, Thyme of different sorts might be planted.

It is an excellent plan, where there is room for it, to arrange one side or end of the garden with ups and downs, like a rock-garden, so that the rock-loving Herbs can root and spread about as they do in nature. A good depth of earth must be given them, quite three feet of it, into which the roots can dive.

We may add that the fortunate possessor of a Herb-garden finds it an ideal refuge for any of the odds and ends of plants that interest him, or that he meets with abroad and wants to experiment with. Many things can find a home in it that would not be sure of a welcome anywhere else— things rare, curious, or unfamiliar, that we like to watch over ourselves. Here, too, we may enjoy such old-fashioned Roses as were valued for their

Carraway

Tarragon

Sorrel

Balm

Alcanet

Mints

Rue

Borage

Peppermint

Rock Camomile

Parsley

Silver Thyme

Purple Sage

Marigold

Fennel

Purple Thyme

Chives

HERB-BORDERS IN JUNE

(Page 13)

sweetness, and are banished in these days, when, owing a good deal to the demands of Flower-shows, size, form, and colour are put before fragrance. Who is going to make a pound of pot-pourri (worth having) out of a whole tentful of fashionable Roses? In the Herb-garden we would have the Moss-Rose, the Damask-Rose, and the Cabbage-Rose. The Cabbage-Rose makes the best rose-water, and the Wild-Briar, or Dog-Rose, is one of the most valuable for its curative qualities. Musk is another plant it is difficult to find nowadays with the same lovely scent that once made it so refreshing and delightful. We might try to secure some Musk of the right sort, and give that, too, a safe corner in the Herb-garden. And why should we not have Sweetbriar? If we do, we must remember it hates formality and confinement. Give it the wildest and most open place; Sweetbriar makes a good hedge.

The size and shape of the garden are points which no one but the owner can decide. It may be said, however, that no Herb-garden is too small to be interesting, and none too large to be easily filled. That good old gardener, Parkinson, in the year 1656 wrote wisely on this head: 'Yet I persuade myself that gentlemen of the better sort and quality

3

will provide such a parcel of ground to be laid out for their garden, and in such convenient manner as may be fit or answerable to the degree they hold. To prescribe one form for every man to follow were too great presumption and folly.'

The difficulties that beset the maker of a Herb-garden are neither those of soil nor site. They lie in a very different direction. You cannot always get the Herbs you want. And why? Because they are not on the market. The common kinds are, of course, to be bought from any florist; but there is not much demand even for them, and now and again disappointment may await us over what would appear such a simple matter as getting Camomile-plants, for instance. Thinking to do better in France, we entered into correspondence with a famous French firm, who sent us an enchanting catalogue of *Plantes Aromatiques*. But it turned out that hardly any of them were in stock for us to see, though all could be procured if we wished. So we decided to order seeds and plants in England. The best English firms are always in · communication with those abroad, and are generally able and pleased to assist the collector. Fellow-gardeners are kind in sparing parts of their treasures; sometimes a cottage-garden will be a mine of homely wealth, and exchanges can be made—a pleasant way of adding to our store. For the rest, there are the fields and hedgerows to ransack. Luck is the only assistance that remains to be noted ; it generally comes to the enterprising.

Enclosed and special gardens are now a fashion of the day. We hear of Blue Gardens, of White Gardens, of Wild Gardens, even of Cactus Gardens. It is the Herb-garden that is generally left out. Is it not a pity ? 'The garden,' says the writer we have quoted at the head of this chapter, 'should be something without and beyond nature, a page from an old romance, a scene in fairyland, a gateway through which imagination, lifted above the sombre realities of life, may pass into a world of dreams.' More than any other kind of garden does the Herb-garden lead us into a region of romance, of mystery and sweet remembrance, yet withal there is a common-sense side to it whose usefulness is not to be denied.

Whichever side appeals to us, there will be charm. One thing is certain, however. If we want our Herb-garden to be really interesting, to be something more and better than a mere adjunct to the kitchen-garden, we must be prepared to give it a good measure of personal attention, searching out the plants we want ourselves, and not minding how much trouble we take to get them. It is not a question simply of ordering and payment. But no true gardener is afraid of difficulties; they do but enhance the pleasure.

Hoping they may be of some assistance to the beginner, we have drawn up a few tables, which will be found at the end of the book. They give lists of the Herbs we think interesting, and the best times for planting or sowing them. Questions of interest, however, vary so much, according to people's tastes, that a few remarks are added descriptive of each, which may be a guide in deciding what to order. We have already said how helpful our English florists and nurserymen are in getting plants and seeds that seem a little out of reach. There is no need to mention them by name; we all have our favourites, but we will give the names and addresses of two French firms highly to be recommended, in case there are any who would like to try their luck abroad. They are Cayeux et Le Clerc, Quai de la Mégisserie, Paris, and Léon Chenalt, Orleans.

In the matter of when to plant I should like to add that, in spite of what the books say, and in defiance of all the grammars of gardening, no one need be afraid of planting anything at any time, if only sufficient care is taken. I have done the rashest things myself with perfect success. For instance, you see some plant you covet very much in a neighbour's garden. 'I will send you a root of that in the autumn—no use moving it now.' This is what is said to you as a small sprig of it is handed over just to look at. 'Take care of that little bit and plant it,' is our advice. Ten to one a morsel of root is clinging to it; anyway, most likely it will grow. In this way we have secured many treasures. This is how I got my precious plant of pure white Thyme, that survived a week of hotel life in London, and was given me (the tiniest scrap of it) at Midsummer, while the plant was in full bloom.

ANNUAL AND BIENNIAL POT-HERBS: TENDER

HOREHOUND
(On the left), from which Horehound beer is brewed

PURSLANE
(With red succulent stalk)

CHAPTER III

‘ Come, buy my knotted Marjoram, ho !’
The Cries of London.

‘ Here’s flowers for you,
Hot Lavender, Mints, Savory, Marjoram.’
Winter’s Tale.

MANY of the most useful of kitchen Herbs are grown from seed. They may be either annuals or biennials. We take the annuals first, and will begin with a few of the tender ones. In their native country several of these plants would be perennials, but because they cannot stand our winters and are killed by frost we have to treat them as annuals. The tender annuals include Sweet Marjoram, *Origanum Marjorana ;* Sweet Green Basil, *Ocymum Basilicum ;* Bush Sweet Basil, *Ocymum minimum ;* and Summer Savory, *Satureia hortensis.* Also the less familiar Purslanes—the Green Purslane, *Portulaca oleracea*; and the Golden Purslane, *Portulaca sativa*.

The tender annuals will repay the trouble of sowing in a hot-bed about the end of March, and removing to a warm border in May, when they should be set out—the Marjoram and Summer Savory about six inches apart, and the Sweet and Bush Basils about a foot or a little less. Some people grow these from the first in the open, but this, as a rule, will only answer in warm and sheltered gardens. Sometimes, however, they do well—provided the soil is kind, and they are given the very sunniest spot—in a cold garden such as my own. We sow about the last week of April or first week of May. Old-fashioned herbalists counsel the sowing of all seeds while the moon is waxing, not waning. We follow this advice, which may account for our seedlings doing so well. Sweet Marjoram, it may be added, seldom gets enough warmth anywhere in England to ripen its seeds; they have to come from abroad.

Sweet Basil likes a rich soil and Sweet Marjoram a sandy one. A rich, light earth suits Summer Savory. As regards shading, watering, and thinning out, all the seedlings want the usual treatment of tender annuals, which is so well known to

every gardener that it need not be particularized.
The same with the Purslanes, of which the Green
Purslane is rather hardier than the Golden. These
two plants want a little more watering than the
other herbs.

The *Sweet* or *Knotted Marjoram* is one of the
delightful kitchen Herbs that has added to man's
happiness.   It is sweet enough and pretty enough
to be put in a nosegay, and so it used to be in
olden time :

> ' Oh, bind them posies of pleasant flowers,
> Of Marjoram, Mint, and Rue.'

Thus runs an old Devonshire song.

In *As You Like It*, Sweet Marjoram is given
its due meed of praise.   ' We may pick a thousand
salads ere we light on such another herb.'   ' Indeed,
sir, she was the Sweet Marjoram of the salad.'
Certainly it is one of the herbs we are sure to
gather a sprig of as we pass it ; and we do not
wonder that our forefathers loved to use it as a
' strewing herb ' before the days of rugs and carpets,
and to put it in their ' sweete bagges and washing-
waters.'   Izaak Walton tells us to use it, along
with a · little bunch of Winter Savory and some
pickled oysters, to dress a pike.'   Of Pot Marjoram

we must speak when we come to talk about perennials.

Sweet Basil is the right Herb for flavouring turtle-soup. It has a warm taste resembling clove, and is a great improvement to sauces and to 'cups.' Two hundred years ago French cooks were just as devoted to it for their *ragoûts* as they are to-day. Why do we so rarely see it in England?

Another form of the Basil plant, *Ocymum sanctum*, is very well known to Anglo-Indians as the Tulasi, a Herb which is held sacred by the Hindoos. A little shrub of it grows out of a square hollow pillar before every Hindoo dwelling. It never looks at all happy or flourishing, though tended every day. Brahmins like to eat a few leaves always after their meals; perhaps they rob the plant too much. No doubt the leaves are excellent for the digestion.

Basil, for all it is used at aldermanic feasts (in soup), has a melancholy association owing, of course, to Isabella and her Basil-pot, with its terrible contents—the decapitated head of her lover, Lorenzo:

> ' She wrapped it up, and for its tomb did choose
> A garden pot, wherein she laid it by,
> And covered it with mould, and o'er it set
> *Sweet Basil*, which her tears kept ever wet.'

No plant that grows, except the Apple, has pro-
voked so much discord and discussion as Basil.
This was because some said it bred serpents, and
you might even get a scorpion in the brain by
smelling it.   Others could not give Basil too good
a character.   A herb so much talked about can
never be put down as insipid ; there must be virtue
in it of one sort or another.   The dried leaves, in
the form of snuff, are said to cure nervous headaches.   In Queen Mary's and Queen Elizabeth's
time little pots of the Basil plant were often given
by the farmers' wives to their landladies and visitors,
a pretty conceit.

Bush Green Basil is a smaller plant than the
Sweet Green Basil. No plant was ever better named.
From the first the seedlings, as they come up, grow
naturally into the most fascinating little shrubs
or bushes, that positively ask to be taken up and
potted.   The strong spiciness of their small green
leaves is quite surprising.   *Ocymum Basilicum*, the
Latin name of the Sweet Green Basil, was given
because ' the smell thereof is fit for a King's house.'
It may interest some to know that it was this herb
which gave the distinctive and peculiarly pleasant
flavour that once made Fetter Lane sausages so
famous.

Sweet Savory takes us back to the modern kitchen. Unconsciously we often enjoy it in the homely sausage, porkpie, or stuffings, where we may be sure it makes for wholesomeness as well as for pleasantness. Or it may be boiled with Peas for Pea-soup, or used to garnish dishes, like Chervil and Parsley. In the fishing season we tire of trout sometimes. Why not make a diversion in the way of dressing it by going to the Herb and kitchen gardens for ' a handful of sliced Horseradish, a handsome little faggot of Rosemary, some Thyme, and a sprig or two of Savory '? This is recommended in Cotton's sequel to the *Compleat Angler*. Major Kenny Herbert tells us to add Summer Savory (*Sarriette*) to Broad Beans when we cook them. After being once cut, the plants produce no succession of shoots ; therefore the whole plant may be pulled up more advantageously than taking cuttings from several. Culpepper considered Summer Savory better than Winter Savory for drying to make conserves and syrups, and to keep by us all the winter.

Of the Purslanes there is less to say. The thick stems are liked by some in salads. The way the plant grows reminds one a little of the Samphire. Of old it was credited with power to cure a vast number of diseases, and was particularly recommended in case of ' blastings by lightning, or planets, or gunpowder.' Did such things commouly happen ? Truth to tell, there is something cooling about the succulent stalks. Many think the Purslanes very homely - looking, but they have their good points, one of which is the rich red colour of the stems. A bit of red among the many grey-green leaves of the Herb-border is always telling.

Briar Roses

Various Mints

Sea-Holly

Elecampane

Mints   Musk   Purple Sage

HERBS BY THE WATERSIDE

ANNUAL AND BIENNIAL POT-HERBS: HARDY

CHAPTER IV

'The even mead, that erst brought sweetly forth
The freckled Cowslip, Burnet and green Clover.'

' The tender tops of Parsley next he culls,
Then the old Rue-bush shudders as he pulls.'

THE hardy pot-herbs grown from seed give no trouble at all, except that of remembering to sow the most useful kinds often enough to keep up a succession. Two of these, Chervil, *Scandix cerefolium*, and Parsley, *Petroselinum sativum*, should always be at hand to pick from, summer and winter. Salad Burnet,[1] *Poterium Sanguisorba*, is a good kitchen Herb, though now neglected. Rampion, *Campanula rapunculus*, is somehow growing into favour again, and the seeds are not difficult to get. Marigold, *Calendula officinalis*, and Borage, *Borago officinalis*—one for its petals, the other for its leaves—have been greatly esteemed in cooking

[1] Really a perennial, but we grow it with the annuals and biennials.

35

and in salads; their gaily coloured flowers are a
fine set-off to the Herb-borders. Skirrets, *Sium
Sisarum*, is a Herb that is cultivated occasionally,
but more as a curiosity than for anything else.

Chervil, one of our most fascinating and service-
able kitchen Herbs, is but rarely seen in England,
though in France it is as common as Parsley, and
a welcome change from that herb which we English
seem to pin all our faith on, why, I know not.
Chervil is quite as hardy and just as easy to grow;
indeed, it comes up much quicker. The plants
remain where sown, and are never transplanted.
If the seedlings spring up too thickly, a slight
thinning will be necessary, and in dry weather a
little watering. Should successive crops be wanted,
we may sow any time between the end of February
and August. August and September sowings can
be used the same autumn and winter. Protection
will be wanted against frost: just a reed hurdle, or
hoops with matting over, or a box-frame. The
proper time for gathering is when the leaves
(bright green and curly) are three or four inches
high. They must be cut off close, when they will
soon shoot up again. The flavour of Chervil is
much milder than that of Parsley, and the young
leaves are excellent in soups and salads. As a

garnish it is even more decorative than our old friend Parsley, but I cannot claim that it is so lasting.

Of *Parsley*, that Prince of biennial Herbs, need much be said? Do we not all know its dawdling way of not coming up, till we are tired of waiting for it? We are well aware of what it has been doing—taking journeys to the Lower Regions and back. It is best to have two sowings of Parsley every year, one in March and one in June, for cooks are always clamouring for it. We must protect it in winter, so as to have it always ready; but Parsley is one of those plants which the hardier you make it the better it is. If a sowing is made in August, and a frame placed over the bed, a good supply can be maintained throughout the winter.

It likes a deep soil, not too rich, and a little soot agrees with it; but Parsley is a rogue and vagabond. Plant him where you will, he likes to go his own way. My very finest Parsley-beds come up of themselves, sometimes on a bank, sometimes in odd corners of the flower or kitchen garden. Here the Herb will flourish, no matter what the soil. In Suffolk an old belief exists that to insure the Herb coming up double, Parsley-seed must be sown on Good Friday. It is also thought very unlucky to transplant Parsley or to meddle with its roots.

Bruised Parsley-seeds are said to be a cure for ague, and taking Parsley in excess to impair the eyesight. An incomprehensible proverb has it that ' Fried Parsley brings a man to his saddle and a woman to her grave.'

Garden Parsley was not cultivated in England until the second year of King Edward VI.'s reign, but no Herb has been so popular with the English people. The different kinds of curled Parsley now to be bought are a triumph of cultivation. Thirty-seven varieties are described in the *Royal Horticultural Society's Journal for* 1909. The old Greeks and Romans who used to make crowns and garlands of this Herb would have revelled in them. The handsome, frilly foliage has another merit: it cannot be mistaken for that of the poisonous Fool's Parsley, a wild plant with smooth plain leaves, a good deal resembling gardeners' Parsley.

Burnet is a pot-herb Sir Francis Bacon loved the smell of so much that he advised its culture along with ' Wild Thyme and Water-Mint' for the pleasure of its scent alone. Whether also as a flavouring for the ' cool tankard' we know not, but this was how it was used in far older times than his; hence its Latin name, *poterium*. The young leaves have something of the flavour of cucumber, and a few of them added to a cup of wine ' helpe to make the heart merrie.'

We scarcely ever see or hear of Burnet now. A chalky soil is very congenial to this Herb.

Rampion should be thinly sown in April or May in rather shady borders. It is not a plant that is commonly seen in England, but in a lovely garden of the Midlands I found a long, long bed of it growing in deep, rich, well-worked earth near a wall. The gardener said, when large enough, he thins the young plants out to about five or six inches apart. The root should be fit for use from November to April. Sometimes it is eaten raw, sometimes boiled for winter salads, and occasionally the leaves are eaten. Major Kenny Herbert (and who understands the cooking of Herbs if he does not?) says they are good eaten as spinach. Why not poach our eggs on some and give ourselves the treat of a new dish? If we grow the Herb for the sake of the root, we must not allow the Rampion to flower. The bell-shaped blue blossoms are pretty; and so far we have cared only for the flowers, and let the roots alone. These will want earthing up several inches on each side, to blanch them, if they are destined for the table. One of Grimm's prettiest fairy tales is written round the Rampion, *Rapunzel;* but, presumably because in England we do not know the plant very well, the translators call it Lettuce.

The cheerful Marigold grows anywhere and seeds itself. We can have either the single or double variety. For cookery, some say the single is the best, but we find the petals of both sorts taste and smell much the same. At one time whole barrels of the golden petals were stored and sold for winter use. 'No broth is well made without dried Marigolds,' was the idea, but Charles Lamb speaks of 'detestable Marigolds floating in the pail' to poison it, and we can well imagine it would not be difficult to overdo such a strong flavour. So far as I am aware, we do not use Marigolds for our soups in England nowadays; but Miss Edgworth's 'Simple Susan' added a few petals as a finishing touch to the broth she had made for her mother. Dr. Fernie says the flowers of Marigold were greatly in request by American doctors during the Civil War, and modern doctors frequently use a lotion made of Marigold for sprains and wounds. As children, the single Mari-

ANISE IN FLOWER AND SEED

(Page 47)

An aromatic herb, from which the famous aniseed is taken, and used for medicinal purposes and for drag-hunts.

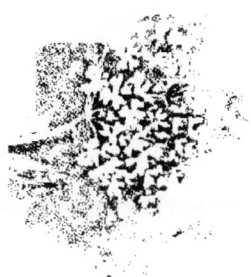

golds used to disappoint us dreadfully by closing at night-time, and so spoiling the effect of nose-gays we had made of them, but poets have always seen the picturesqueness of this childish habit :

> ' The Marigold that goes to bed wi' the sun,
> And with him rises weeping.'

> ' Open afresh your round of starry folds,
>   Ye ardent Marigolds !
> Dry up the moisture from your golden lids,
>   For great Apollo bids
> That in these days your praises should be sung.'

' *Borage* for courage !' So runs the old proverb. Once sown, you need never sow Borage again ; like the Marigolds, it takes care of itself. The starry blue flowers with a cunning dot of black in them are delightful. Blue flowers often have a beauty-patch of black like this. The rough green leaves give an etherealized flavour of cucumber to claret and other cups, and the flowers offer honey to the bees. Our great-great-grandmothers loved to preserve the flowers and candy them for sweet-meats.

Skirrets, a perennial best grown as an annual, can be raised from seed, or, once established, from offsets of the roots, but it is so old-fashioned that

seeds are difficult to get.   Its tubers were eaten
either roasted or boiled.   History tells us that the
Emperor Tiberias valued it so much that he
accepted it as tribute, and it was conveyed to him
from Gelduba, a castle on the River Rhine.   In
Scotland the plant is known as Crummock.

There are many salad Herbs we can grow from
seed, if we like, such as Corn-salad or Lamb's
Lettuce, in France called *Mâches,* or by the
peasants *Tusette.*   It is almost always served with
turkey.   Chicory, *Cichorium Intybus,* is a good
Christmas salad, and should be sown in June ; the
leaves will furnish the salad-bowl, and the roots can
be blanched and eaten like Seakale, but these
plants seem more in place in the kitchen-garden.
Nor do we care to grow Nasturtiums among the
Herbs : they are so common everywhere and so
greedy of room ; but there was a time when they
were as much prized for their usefulness as for their
gay flowers ; the ' nuts,' or capsules, were a substitute for capers, and infusions of the plant were
considered aromatic, cordial, and antiscorbutic ; the
petals, too, went into salads.

In fine summers we always save our seeds, but
never grudge the expense of buying fresh.   The
cost is but trifling, and warmer climes have better

chances of ripening seeds than we have. On the other hand, home-saved seeds are never stale—you can depend on that. Any of the high-class florists will get seeds from Paris or elsewhere, if requested.

Sometimes we have recourse to the old-fashioned homely way of ' mothering ' the seeds that fall— that is to say, leaving them where they lie, and covering them and feeding them during the winter. These seedlings often make the best and strongest plants, also the earliest, but in very cold springs they may suffer. Many other plants besides those named can be grown from seed if we like—in fact, pretty well all of them ; but some of the Herbs advertised in catalogues as raised from seed would be better if grown from slips or divisions of the roots.

The general scheme of seed-sowing is so well described in Tusser's *Five Hundred Points of Good Husbandry*, that we cannot refrain from quoting a few verses of it :

' In March and in April, from morning till night,
In sowing and setting good housewives delight ;
To have in a garden or other like plot
To trim up their house and to furnish their pot.

'Time and ages to sow or to gather be bold,
　But set to remove when the weather be cold :
　Cut all things or gather, the moon on the wane,
　But sow in increasing, or give it its bane.

' Now sets do ask watering with pot or with dish,
　New-sown do not so, if ye do as I wish :
　Through cunning with dibble, rake, mattock and spade,
　By line and by level the garden is made.

' Who soweth too lateward, hath seldom good seed,
　Who soweth too soon, little better shall speed ;
　Apt time and the seasons, so diverse to hit,
　Set aiér and layer, help practice and wit.'

AROMATIC HERBS GROWN FOR
THEIR SEEDS

CHAPTER V

'How do the tiny seeds transform
To living gold the leaden sod ?
How is the dead made quick and warm ?
Oh, mystic alchemy of God !

'We know not by what charm 'tis done,
This miracle of summer hours ;
But yet of earth, the rain, and sun,
Are made the living golden flowers.'

SOME Herbs are precious for the sake of their roots,
some for the sake of their leaves, some for their
flowers, and others for the sake of their seeds.
To a group of aromatic Herbs of this sort the
present chapter shall be devoted.

The growing of plants from seed is one of the
gardener's greatest pleasures. He is the first to
see the small green leaves or earliest spikes that
part the mould. How greatly is the interest of
this yearly miracle enhanced, when the plants

whose shoots we watch for are strangers to us! Few, I imagine, have the least idea what Dill, Coriander, Caraway, or Anise look like when growing. Yet these four aromatic Herbs, although of Eastern origin, do well in English gardens if given a sunny place. They grew quite happily in my breezy garden, where they flowered and went to seed.

Dill, *Anethum graveolens*, turned out to be a lively-looking upright sort of plant, with umbels of pretty yellow flowers. The taste of the seeds is an odd blend of different spices. The name Dill is said to be derived from a Norse word that means to 'dull,' or from the Saxon verb *dilla*, to 'lull,' because the seeds are soporific, and used to be given to little babies to make them sleep.

Dill, for infants, is still in fashion. Our village chemist tells us he is always selling it in 'pennorths' for mothers to keep their babies quiet with; but if I set up a still to make Dill-water for them myself, I shall be prosecuted! In cookery, the leaves may be added to fish or mixed with pickled cucumber to 'give the cold fruit a pretty spicie taste.' Of old it was a favourite herb in magic:

'Here holy Vervain, and here Dill,
'Gainst witchcraft much availing.'

The plant is largely grown in the East Indies, where they call it *Soyah*, and use it both as a pot-herb and in physic; very likely in incantations also.

Coriander, *Coriandrum sativum*, grows about the same height as Dill, and the flower-heads are of much the same size. The two plants look well side by side, for they bloom at the same time. Coriander flowers are delicately pretty, of a pale mauve colour, almost white. But the best time for Coriander is when the seeds are ripe and everybody is asked to taste them and say what they are reminded of. The flavour seems familiar, yet you cannot put a name to it. It is those funny little rough-coated pink or white sugar-plums found in the best mixed sweets. When you have done with the sugar and got down to the seed, you know what Coriander tastes like. Extremely good. A lady told me that a Spanish cook she had, positively refused to make a curry without Coriander seeds. They are perfectly round, like tiny balls. The manna so mysteriously rained from Heaven was compared to Coriander—

' That hangs on slightest threads her trembling seeds.'

As soon as the seeds are ripe they fall, leaving

only the bare stalks. The seed-clusters are very symmetrical.

Caraway, *Carum Carui*, does best when treated as a biennial, and should be sown in autumn. The foliage so much resembles Carrot that it is not surprising to hear that the roots are sometimes boiled and eaten as Carrots. Dr. Fernie advises all good housewives to keep both Coriander and Caraway seeds in their cupboards. German housekeepers never fail to do so. With the Germans Caraway is exceedingly popular. The peasants flavour their cheese, soups, and bread with it, and add it to their national *Sauerkraut*. Like the Russians, they use it in *Kummel*. We English like it fairly well in seed-cakes and in Caraway comfits, and in some country places people pound up the bruised seeds with the crumb of a hot new loaf and a little spirit to moisten. This compound is supposed to cure the most frantic earaches. We have been told that at some of the old-fashioned London Livery Dinners little saucers filled with Caraway seeds are still served with roasted apples—a truly Shakespearian idea. 'You shall see my orchard,' says Justice Shallow, 'where in an arbour we will eat a pippin of last year's graffing, with a dish of caraways.'

There is plenty of honey in Caraway blossoms, but the tiny florets on the flat discs are so shallow that only certain insects can get at it. Sir John Lubbock watched a dinner-party that went on one summer's day in the Caraway bed; he counted that out of fifty-five visitants, one moth, nine bees, twenty-one flies, and twenty-four midges made up the company.

Anise, *Pimpinella Anisum*, as it flowered and went to seed, was one of the Herbs we enjoyed most, partly because it is such a dainty, white-flowered little plant, and also because, having always heard so much of 'Aniseed,' as it is called, both in physic and at drag-hunts, we were curious to see how the plant looked when growing. It has secondary feather-like leaflets of bright green, which are a great addition to its personal appearance, and give the plant its title—Pimpinella, from *bipinella*. It is an odd literary mistake to make Aniseed a plural noun. There is a book called *The Englishman's Doctor*, wherein it says, 'Some anny seeds be sweet and some bitter.'

At first sight, there does not seem to be much connection between Anise and wedding-cakes, but Dr. Fernie finds one. The mustacæ, or spiced cakes of the Romans, introduced at the close of a

rich entertainment to prevent indigestion, consisted
of meal with Anise, Cumin, and other aromatics.
Such a cake was commonly brought in at the end
of a marriage feast, and hence the bride-cake of
modern times.   The least suspicion of Anise among
the spices in a wedding-cake of these days would
be thought dreadful.   Tastes have changed so
much, or is it possible that people were strong-
minded enough at one time not to object to the
addition of certain unpalatable ingredients if convinced they would do them good?   In the East,
as everybody knows, Anise, with other aromatic
Herbs, was used in part payment of taxes: ' Ye pay
tithe of Mint, Anise, and Cummin.'

Cumin, *Cuminum Cyminum*, or Cummin, as it is
spelt in the Bible, is a Herb which *not* to have in
our garden is considered one of its failures.   It is
invariably asked for during that pleasant idle hour
between church and luncheon, when most people
wander round their own gardens and each other's
gardens making remarks and observing anything
new.   Myrrh and Hyssop are there, and Mint of
course.   Where, then, is the Cumin?   The seeds
are difficult to get, as it is so seldom grown in
England.   Gerarde says they have the same virtue
as the Caraway.   ' Cumin good for eyes,' writes

Spenser. The plant has jagged leaves and red or purplish flowers. As a physic it has been considered from the earliest times to possess the power of making healthy faces pale ; also of curing pallor brought about by illness. As a love-potion it prevents fickleness. An invaluable Herb this !

PERENNIAL KITCHEN HERBS

POT MARJORAM, PINK AND WHITE

CHAPTER VI

PERENNIAL KITCHEN HERBS

' Herbs, too, she knew, and well of each could speak,
    That in her garden sipped the silvery dew ;
Where no vain flower disclosed a gaudy streak,
    But herbs for use, and physic not a few.'

OUR nine most useful perennial kitchen Herbs are : Mint, *Mentha viridis ;* Sage, *Salvia officinalis ;* Common Thyme, *Thymus vulgaris ;* Lemon Thyme, *Thymus citriodorus ;* Winter Savory, *Satureia montana ;* Pot Marjoram, *Origanum Onites ;* Tarragon, *Artemisia Dracunculus ;* Fennel, *Fœniculum vulgare ;* and Sorrel, *Rumex.* Beside these Herbs, there are two more we ought to have, because, although they have fallen out of use in our time, they are well worth growing for one reason or another. They are Sweet Cicely, *Myrrhis odorata,* and Alecost, or Costmary, *Balsamita vulgaris.* Mints will have a chapter to themselves, so we begin with Sage.

Sage will grow anywhere, and is one of the few Herbs that still belong to modern everyday life. Still do the cooks ask for it and the gardeners bring it in; still does it mitigate for mortal man the richness of pork, ducks, and geese. 'How can a man die who has Sage in his garden?' is a proverb of Arabia.

> ' He that would live for aye
> Must eat of Sage in May,'

is an English one. They show how the Herb has been valued both East and West. The Chinese cannot imagine why Europeans like their Tea-leaves better than home-grown Sage - leaves for brewing. Time was when exchanges were made between the Dutch and Chinese—four pounds of tea for one pound of Sage ! Sage, they say, makes a capital gargle, and the smell of it alone is sometimes strong enough to make the patient giddy.

Along with the Green Sage we like to grow the Purple; both make nice hardy plants if cut back now and then. There is a variegated Sage, too, of lovely colours. Meadow or Wild Sage, *Salvia sclarea*, never seen in gardens nowadays, is known about the country-side as Clary or Clear-eyes, and at one time was as much valued as the garden kind. Its names explain the reason why.

It has also been called *Oculus Christi*. Occasionally the whole young plant would be eaten, either boiled or fried in sweet butter with sugar and the juice of oranges or lemons. We have it on good authority that George Whitefield, when at Oxford (1733), lived almost entirely on Sage-tea, with sugar and coarse bread.

Thyme! What a lovely thing to write about, to think of! Lemon Thyme, so clean-smelling, so fragrant, such a pleasant seasoning ; Wild Thyme on the bank, 'with oxlips and the nodding violet'; Common Thyme on heath and down, that spreads the softest carpet foot of man can tread, and helps along with the small striped snails to make the plump Down-sheep into such delicious mutton. I am glad to know that there are few gardens in England without a patch of Thyme. The larger the patch the better. There is a lovely little dwarf Thyme, too, with flowers of crimson, that loves to creep about among the stones. I think it is either *Thymus montana* or *Thymus Corsicus*. This and the Golden Thyme and the Silver Thyme and a variegated form of the Lemon-scented Thyme are all desirable.

Their culture is as easy as possible. Cuttings and slips are the usual method of propagation;

but if a good large bed has to be made, the best
plan is to scatter seed thinly in a light dry soil,
early in April, not covering too deeply. The young
plants will soon be up, when they can be removed
to permanent quarters, which must be sunny.
Lemon Thyme is more robust than the green-leafed
kind, and keeps its foliage better in the winter. If
the soil we give it does not seem to suit it very well,
a little road-sand or sweepings will be welcomed—
a gritty soil it will root into quickly. It is thought
that Lemon Thyme when raised from seed has not
so agreeable a perfume as that which is raised from
cuttings or by division.

Winter Savory will grow either from seed or
slips. It is a woodier and more bushy plant than
the Summer Savory, and flowers contentedly
among the stones of a rockery. Thus have I seen
it in the Old Physic Garden, Chelsea. Gardeners
still have faith in the virtue of its leaves and sprigs
to cure wasp and bee stings. It is safer to plant
this herb in a poor soil than a rich one. In rich
earth the plants imbibe too much moisture to
stand the severity of our winters. In soil that suits
it Winter Savory makes a good-sized shrub.

Pot Marjoram, like Thyme, to be at its best
should have ample space to spread in. The most

beautiful patches I have seen were in a Norfolk garden that was large enough for the luxury of growing such plants in masses.   A wide border of the kitchen-garden was given up entirely to Marjoram, two kinds of it growing side by side— one with flowers of the usual tender pink, the other with flowers that were white.   This white Marjoram is rarely seen in gardens ; possibly it was a reversion to some wild form.   I have never seen it but that once, and cannot hear of it in other places. Will it come true another year ?   That is the in- teresting question.   We are glad that both kinds were sketched for us while they were in bloom.

One could not easily forget these lovely borders, the unassuming charm of their soft colouring, the dainty sweetness of their scent.   Over them, in the warm summer sunshine, brown bees were drowsily humming, and silken wings from flower to flower were fluttering—from pink to white, and then to pink again :

> ' With light and butterfly the world did seem
>   To flicker and flit,
>   As if the Maker slept and in a dream
>   Imagined it.'

This is the way to grow sweet Herbs if you really mean to enjoy them.   *Origanum* is a word that means 'joy of the mountains,' and of old those who mourned their loved ones were comforted if Marjoram grew wild upon their graves. It meant that those who had passed away were happy.

Tarragon is another Herb that loves warmth and sunshine. Those who have it in their gardens (and it is a positive duty to do so) can enjoy homemade *Vinaigre d'Estragon*, which is excellent; also they will possess the one and only correct flavouring for *Sauce Tartare*. It is as well to warn the cooks who have been given the key of the Herb-garden to be cautious how they use Tarragon. The taste is so strong and peculiar, and if a chance leaf finds its way into the bunch of Sweet Herbs used for soup, great consternation will result at dinner-time.

Fennel immediately suggests boiled mackerel. At one time Fennel sauce was *de rigueur* with it. But is it now? Fennel has fallen strangely from its former high estate. Many a kitchen-garden of these days knows it not. What would King Edward I. have said to such degenerate ways? He and his household consumed it at the rate of eight and a half pounds for one month. The poor used to eat it when hungry, and it made them feel satisfied ; fat people ate it to make themselves thin ; blind people ate it to restore their sight, having observed serpents did this, or so we are told. Quantities of poetry have been written about this Herb, with its odd strong taste, its tall straggling branches, its bright golden flowers. This is part of what the gentle poet of America had to say about it :

> ' Above the lowly plants it towers,
>   The fennel with its yellow flowers,
>   And in an earlier age than ours
>   Was gifted with the wondrous powers
>   Lost vision to restore.

> ' It gave new strength and fearless mood,
>   And gladiators, fierce and rude,
>   Mingled it in their daily food ;
>   And he who battled and subdued
>   The wreath of fennel wore.'

Less striking is this Herb than many another plant, yet round ' the yellowing fennel run to seed,' were woven some of Browning's most subtle thoughts. Evidently there is something wanting in people who are blind to the fascinations of Fennel.

There is another Fennel, known as *Finocchio* or Florence Fennel, the swollen stem bases of which are boiled and form a favourite dish in Italy.

English people have begun to like it, and there is no difficulty in getting seeds of the plant.

Sorrel is so much of a vegetable in appearance that we wonder why it should be reckoned as a Herb, and usually relegated to the Herb-garden. There are two kinds—Garden Sorrel and French Sorrel. *Oseille large de Belleville* is said to be the very best sort for eating, as it is not too acid. The true French *Soupe aux Herbes* is never made without Sorrel. When no apples are forthcoming for apple-sauce, Sorrel-leaves are a good substitute. All the Sorrels are terrible spreaders, and must be kept in check, or they will overrun everything else.

Myrrhis odorata, or *Sweet Cicely*, is a Herb of the past, and it surprises us to learn that its leaves were at one time liked in salads. They taste like paregoric. But the plant is pretty enough for the flower-garden, where it sometimes has a place. The spreading verdant foliage is finely cut, like that of ferns. The seeds are full of oil, have a pleasanter taste than the leaves, and in olden times were crushed and used to scent and polish furniture and oaken floors. A curious whiteness is often noticed on the leaves; they look as if white powder had been sprinkled over them. Apparently the

FENNEL

(With yellow blossom)

TARRAGON

(On the right)

From which is made *Vinaigre d'Estragon*

foliage thus marked is healthy, so I cannot account for the whiteness.

Costmary, or *Alecost,* is another Herb that is seldom seen or heard of in these days. We have grown it for the last seven years, and it puzzles the most accomplished gardeners who notice it in our borders. It has long, narrow, pale green leaves, finely jagged at the edges and smelling exactly like weak Mint sauce. It has much the same flavour, too, except that it leaves an after-taste of bitterness. Why it so greatly resembles Mint in smell and taste we cannot imagine, as it has no family relationship with Mint whatever, but belongs to another order. Beer and Negus used to be flavoured with it.

> 'Costmary that so likes the cup,
> And with it Pennyroyal.'

Our great-grandmothers loved to tie up bunches of the white Costmary flowers along with Lavender. These they would 'lye upon the toppes of beds, presses, etc., for sweet scent and savours.' Grown in the shade, Costmary goes strongly to leaf, but will not flower.

Perennial Herbs, to be grown successfully, should be lifted and transplanted every three or four years, or, if not transplanted, should each

9

autumn have a good top dressing of rich soil. All those we have been speaking of are quite hardy, except the Tarragon. Please keep a warm corner for this.

TEN KINDS OF MINT

CHAPTER VII

TEN KINDS OF MINT

'Come, buy my Mint, my fine green Mint!
Let none despise the merry, merry cries
Of famous London Town.'

THERE is always a danger when writing on a subject of great interest to ourselves that we may allow it to run away with us and so bore everybody else. I hope this will not be the case with Mints. We cannot help feeling a little proud at having collected ten different varieties. This is not an easy thing to do. It is very doubtful whether any Mints whatever, beyond the ordinary Lamb Mint and a certain variegated Mint which is pretty and attractive enough to go in the flower-garden, could be found among the plants that are advertised in any of the florists' catalogues.

How, then, did we get our ten? Some we found easily, some we hunted for with pains, some were given to us, and some we got by accident.

69

This is the ten we possess: Spear Mint, *Mentha viridis;* Corn-Mint, *M. arvensis;* White Woolly or Horse Mint, *M. sylvestris;* Round-leafed Mint, *M. rotundifolia;* Lemon Mint, *M. citrata;* Curly-leafed Mint, *M. crispus;* Peppermint, *M. piperita;* Water or Hairy Mint, *M. aquatica;* Penny-royal, *Mentha pulegium;* and Cat-Mint, *Nepeta cataria.* There is also a Variegated Mint, which would make eleven if counted.

How do we manage to get Mints by accident? Very easily, if one lives in the country. Cottage gardeners bring queer sorts to sell you, instead of proper Lamb Mint. Instead of grumbling at this, you ask them to spare you a root; then you pay a trifle for it, or make some friendly exchange, and the thing is done. All the Mints are useful, but all are not fit for the table—that is, if you are any way fastidious.

And how are the other Mints collected? Lamb Mint can be bought anywhere. Corn-Mint must be looked for on the edges of cornfields; White Woolly Mint we had to hunt for in damp waste places. The Round-leafed Mint was much more difficult to find, though it grows in similar spots. Lemon Mint was a present; Curly-leafed Mint was also given us. Peppermint was sent to us by mistake; the Variegated Mint we bought, and the common Water Mint required no looking for. Does it not throw itself at our heads, as it were, or rather feet, whenever summer wanderings lead us by running rills, or river-banks, or watery meadows? Here it grows luxuriantly, smelling very strong and nice, suggesting merry picnics and the washing-up of cups and plates.

Spear or Lamb Mint is grown, as a matter of course, in every well-regulated garden. It is too well known to need description, but may we say a word here about Mint sauce? Most of us like it with roast lamb, but do we recognize how wholesome is the Herb we are enjoying? It is a valuable condiment, which helps to make the immature meat less indigestible. 'With bitter herbs shalt thou eat it.' All the Jewish mandates were so sensible. Remembering this one, what a halo of interest, almost of romance, is thrown around the twentieth-century dinner-table! At the least, the homely Herb when eaten thus, is a link with the long, long past.

Corn-Mint, like other Mints, has the power of preventing milk from curdling, and I have heard that cows which feed on it make trouble for the dairy-maids, who cannot imagine why the milk will

not turn into cheese.　This anti-curdling property
of Mint may be the secret of its success in medicines.
Preparations of Mint are very useful when people
are put on milk diet, also for little children.　Mints
are still used in the prescriptions of modern doctors,
Peppermint for the grown-up people, and Spear
Mint, being milder, for the little ones.

The *White Woolly Mint* is the finest of the
family.　It has downy foliage, very white on the
under side, fine large spires of lilac flowers that
spring from the main stem, a free way of growing.
and a very strong taste and smell.　All the Mints
like plenty of moisture, but I have seen this plant
look quite splendid on the Herb-border of a sunny
walled garden in Norfolk.　We took his picture.
It was a Norfolk man, too, who said he thought
the Woolly Mint made the best Mint sauce.
Certainly it would not lack flavour.　He would
have been a kindred spirit with Seneca, who, I
believe by his own wish, perished in a bath scented
with this particular Herb.

Lemon Mint, if not so handsome as the Woolly
Mint, is by far the most fascinating of all the
Mints we know.　The leaves are variegated, dark
green striped with lemon colour, and they have the
most delicious and lasting perfume imaginable ;

WHITE-WOOLLY MINT,
OR HORSE-MINT

very distinctive, too, less sweet than the scent of Balm, but much more refreshing.

'The juyce of the gentler tops' of this Mint, mixed with orange juice and a little sugar, made a favourite conserve. It is recommended by Culpepper, who speaks of the plant as Orange Mint.

Peppermint is one of the most popular Herbs in the garden, for anyone need but pick a leaf and smell it, and at once he knows what it is. If people only knew how good the fresh green leaves are, when bruised and laid upon the aching part to cure nervous headaches, the plant would be liked even better than it is. There is such a curious hot-coldness about Peppermint; it diffuses warmth, yet with it a strange numbness which is soothing. The flowery tops of all Mints contain a certain portion of camphor. Peppermint is responsible for that modern comfort, menthol—modern to us, that is. The Japanese enjoyed its blessing two hundred years ago, and carried it about in silver boxes hanging from their girdles. Peppermint can easily be distinguished at sight from Spear Mint by its leaves being stalked, also by having a more purplish tinge of colour.

Water Mint, the commonest of our English Mints, is often spoken of as wild Peppermint, and

it has much the same smell and properties. It
is remarkable that such water-loving plants as
Mints should be aromatic. As a rule, aromatic
plants belong to hot, dry places. The essential
oil in their leaves serves, Professor Tyndall tells us,
to protect them from the intense heat of the sun;
the passage of the heat rays is hindered. The late
Professor made a series of experiments, too, as to
the absorption of heat by odorous vapours. Air
scented with patchouli had thirty times the cooling
effect of fresh air, and cassia had actually one
hundred and nine times the effect. Do we not all
know how a spray of perfume diffused about a room
will cool it? Rowing men, when resting in some
leafy Peppermint-scented backwater on a hot day,
must have noticed what a cooling, refreshing influence is somehow spread around. Let me ask them
next time this happens to give a grateful thought
to the wild Mints. I believe they deserve it.

Pennyroyal grows quite differently from the
other Mints. It creeps about close to the ground,
and used to be known as 'Lurk-in-the-Ditch,' or
' Run - by - the - Ground.' 'Pudding - Grass ' was
another name for it, because it was used in hogs'
puddings. Gerarde, whose garden at Holborn
flourished in Queen Elizabeth's time, said: 'It
groweth naturally wilde in the Common near

London, called Miles End, about the holes and ponds thereof in many places, from whence poore women bring plentie to sell in London markets.' Trails of it, dried and thrown by handfuls into stagnant water, were supposed to purify and make it fit for drinking. Sailors, therefore, were glad to buy the Herb and use it when at sea. In hot countries Pennyroyal is thought to be a good protection from mosquitoes, and the royal way it keeps off other insects is responsible for its Latin name, *Mentha pulegium.* In Italy it counteracts the evil-eye, and in Sicily is hung on Fig-trees to prevent the Figs from falling before they are ripe. Here, too, the children put Pennyroyal among the green things that line their Christmas crêches, and believe that exactly at midnight on Christmas Eve the little plants burst into buds that will be in full bloom on Christmas Day. Pliny came to the conclusion, after much consultation, that a chaplet of Pennyroyal worn on the head was far better than one of Roses to relieve giddiness. In Elizabethan days the Herb was thought worthy of a place in the posies that were given and accepted by true lovers:

'Peniriall is to print your love
So deep within my heart,
That when you look this nosegay on
My pain you may impart,

And when that you have read the same,
   Consider well my woe—
Think ye then how to recompense
Even him that loves you so !'

Cat-Mint is the last of our ten different Mints, and hardly seems as if it were in its right place even at the end, for it is not a mere pot-herb, like the other Mints.   So many people grow it in their gardens for the sake of its pretty blue flowers, that we forget to reckon it as a Herb at all ; yet there was a time, before the use of tea from China, when our English peasantry were in the habit of brewing Cat-Mint tea, which they said was quite as pleasant and a good deal more wholesome.   Perhaps it was.   Anyhow, Ellen Montgomery of *The Wide, Wide World* made Cat-Mint tea for Miss Fortune when she was ill.   Certainly it is stimulating. The root, when chewed, is said to make the most gentle person fierce and quarrelsome, and a legend is extant of a certain hangman who could never screw up his courage to the point of hanging anybody till he had partaken of it.   That such a meek and gentle-looking Herb should be possessed of such alarming qualities is surprising.

Cats are much too fond of this plant.   Not for nothing is it called by the English Cat-Mint, and by the French *Herbe aux chats*.   In the Chelsea

Physic-garden, surrounded as it is with houses, vagrant cats would soon destroy the Herb altogether if it were not protected by barricades.

> 'If you set it, the cats will eate it ;
> If you sow it, the cats won't know it.'

This old rhyme is all very well, but the cats would know it as soon as it was up. They roll in it, browse on it, and cannot leave it alone. Rats, on the other hand, dislike the plant particularly, and will not approach it even when driven by hunger.

'If the green Herb (not the dry) be boiled in wine, and the face washed with it, blue and black marks will disappear, and black scars will become well coloured.' This is the advice of an old herbalist, who, if he did not claim so many other virtues for this Herb, would be more worthy of credence as to this one.

Cat-Mint, by the way, does not demand moisture in the same way as the other Mints. It will grow on heaths and uplands, and make itself quite happy among plants in the rock-garden. The wild form of the Herb is known about the country-side as Calamint.

Mint has been called in France *Menthe de Notre Dame*, in Italy *Erba Santa Maria*, and in Germany *Frauen Münze*. In the days when the floors of

churches were strewn with sweet and bitter herbs—
a pleasant, wholesome fashion—Mints were among
the favourites for the purpose.

The cultivation of Mints is very simple. All of
them like plenty of moisture, except Corn-Mint,
which is accustomed to dry fields, and Cat-Mint,
which grows anywhere. Spear Mint, the kitchen
and most useful sort, is liable to be attacked by
rust, so it is a wise precaution to have several
beds of it placed at some distance from each other.
Provided Mint is properly nourished at the root,
it will not want frequent watering; but if not well
fed, the roots will be stunted, the stems wiry, and
the leaves small. In autumn the old growths
should be cut close to the ground. To have really
good Mint it must be transplanted every third
year, or, failing that, a good top dressing of rich
soil must be added. Roots may be divided and
the plants re-arranged either in spring or autumn.
Green Mint is often asked for in early spring, and
it is a good plan to provide this by putting a few
outside runners into pots, and placing them in
bottom heat. Strangely enough, in quite good
gardens there is often a dearth of Mint just when
wanted; but what a disgrace to buy a Herb so
easily cultivated!

A BUNDLE OF BITTER HERBS

WORMWOOD IN FLOWER

From this extremely bitter herb absinthe is made

CHAPTER VIII

A BUNDLE OF BITTER HERBS

'Some Camomile doth not amiss,
    With Savory and some Tansey.'

'Many Herbes and flowers that have small beautie or savour
to commend them have much more good use and vertue.'

WORMWOOD, *Artemisia absinthium ;* Rue, *Ruta
graveolens ;* Camomile, *Anthemis nobilis ;* Horehound, *Marrubium vulgare ;* and Tansy, *Tanacetum
vulgare*—all these are bitter Herbs indeed, but no
Herb-garden would be complete without them :
great is their virtue.

Wormwood, with the exception of Rue, is the
bitterest Herb known ; but everyone must look
on it with interest, if only because of its respon-
sibility for the world-famous absinthe.   In France
whole fields of it are grown for no other object
than the making of this terrible cordial, or poison
—which should we call it ?   The plant is not

poisonous really, but very wholesome. It makes splendid bitters. In a very old-fashioned garden of the Midlands last summer I was pleased to find plenty of Wormwood growing by a sunny wall, and fondly hoped it was a relic of the old days, when kings hid and nuns were walled up in the chimneys of the old manor-house to which the garden belonged. But nothing of the kind. The gardener had planted it with a view to providing his neighbours with good physic for the coming winter. The wild Wormwood, or Mugwort, grows freely on the sea-coast, and is quite common on the cliffs of Norfolk.

Rue is a Herb we must enjoy for the uncommon and lovely colour of its leaves—such a soft bluish-green. Every artist's eye spies it out at once. It is easier to admire the colour than to find the right pigments to reproduce it in a picture. As to its use, cattle-owners and poultry-keepers are well aware of its value as a homely physic, and many of our country-folk still delight in it as a medicine for themselves. An old woman living near our village tells us it is the only remedy that does her any good. She takes it chopped up, between slices of bread and butter. Oddly enough, a young lady who has just been staying with a family in

Germany informs us that Rue sandwiches just like these are quite the fashion with them for afternoon tea!

It is not so very long ago that Rue was strewed about the prisoners' dock when criminal trials were on at the Old Bailey Sessions. As children, we were told by our gardener 'it kept off fleas.' Perhaps the lawyers were of the same opinion. It has always been thought to possess great powers of purification.

> ' What savour is better, if physic be true,
>   For places infected than Wormwood and Rue ?'

Rue was a Herb much used in exorcism, and at the present day in churches abroad we sometimes find branches of it brought in to sprinkle holy water. Some people find the smell of Rue detestable; as a child I could not endure it, but now have grown to think its clean and wholesome bitterness quite pleasing. We love the sturdy little shrub, too, for its hardiness; the bushy small-leafed plants hold their own bravely through all the wintry weather, smiling their blue-green placid smiles unruffled. The flowers of Rue are yellow, and not at all conspicuous.

Camomile has quite a different character. For one thing, the virtue of the plant is in the flowers, not the leaf; anyhow, it is the flowers that are saved and dried to use medicinally. It is extraordinary that nowadays Camomile should be so little valued; there is even some difficulty, as I think I have said before, in getting plants or seeds of it. You may go to florist after florist, and draw a blank as regards Camomile. It is never asked for, they say, so people who want it must exercise patience till some friend comes along who has some, and will spare a root or two.

The flowers are like little Daisies, with a fringe of white florets outside, and yellow discs in the centre. In these discs lies the virtue of the plant. The cultivated Camomile gradually loses the yellow discs, exchanging them for more of the white florets, which makes the blossoms prettier to the eye but useless for physic. The one true and original Camomile grows close to the ground, and when allowed to seed about, makes a soft greensward, which, as Falstaff said, 'the more it is trodden on the faster it grows.' The plant produces but one flower from each stem.

A very clever gardener has told me of the Camomile, that it is an invaluable substitute for grass in arid places—a dry bank, for instance. The colour of its green is vivid and beautiful, quite as fair to look on as the grass of a lawn.   Pieces of it, when first planted, are not very happy, but soon recover, and then spread fast.   I am glad to know that the Camomile we are speaking of is a native of Britain.

We grow another Camomile in the Herb-garden for its beauty ; it has finely cut grey-green foliage and abundant daisy-like flowers.   This is the Rock Camomile, *Anthemis Cupaniana.*   One of our illustrations shows it very well.   It has but little of the Camomile bitter.

There is one remarkable property about the Camomile which some still believe in implicitly— that it is the plants' physician.   Nothing is thought to keep a garden so healthy as plenty of Camomile about ; it will even revive drooping and sickly plants if placed near them.   Some of our villagers, in spite of having let the Camomile die out of their gardens, declare that their parents considered Camomile the best medicine they had.   Besides making tea and poultices, it was smoked in the men's pipes to cure asthma.   Bags stuffed loosely with the flowers and steeped in boiling water relieve neuralgia and have a pleasant aromatic smell that does one good.   The following is a good recipe for making Camomile-tea :   Pour half a pint

of boiling water on half an ounce of the dried
flower-heads, and let this stand for fifteen minutes ;
sweeten with sugar or honey.   A draught of this,
taken at bedtime, is a sure preventive of night-
mare.

Horehound is bitter with quite a different bitterness.   In Norfolk many a cottage garden has its
Horehound corner, and Horehound beer is brewed
and drunk.   Syrup of Horehound is good for
coughs and colds.   We grow it principally because
we like the harmonious colour of the grey-green
stalks and leaves, and often plant it near the rosy-
stemmed Purslane for the sake of contrast.   In
our illustration we have placed a branch of each of
these Herbs side by side.   The Water-Horehound,
or Gipsy-Wort, is found growing on the Norfolk
Broads.   This plant yields a dark dye, used by
gipsies ; hence its name.

Tansy, perhaps the least bitter Herb of the
bunch, is still bitter enough to cause surprise that
Tansy cakes and puddings could ever have been
liked.   Surely wry faces must have been made
over them !   They were eaten, more especially at
Easter-time, as some say, to correct the ill-effects
of a prolonged fish diet.

'Soone at Easter cometh Alleluya,
  With butter, cheese, and a Tansy.'

So runs an old Easter carol. Another song begins thus :

' On Easter Sunday be the pudding seen,
  To which the Tansy lends her sober green.'

We think the Tansy too much of a vagrant to be allowed a footing in the Herb-garden. He looks far more in place out on the common, where he can display his fine array of bright brass buttons to more advantage. Sir James Sawyer says that the oil of Tansy merits a great deal more attention than is now given to it, and might well enter into the composition of toilet vinegars and perfumed salts.

TANSY

A bitter herb, formerly used for Tansy cakes and puddings, which were eaten at Easter-time to correct the ill-effects of a long fish diet.

BULBOUS PLANTS FOR THE HERB-GARDEN

CHAPTER IX

BULBOUS PLANTS FOR THE HERB-GARDEN

' When harvest is gone
Then Saffron comes on ;
A little of ground
Brings Saffron a pound.
The pleasure is fine,
The profit is thine.
Keep colour in drying,
Well used, worth buying.'

BULBOUS plants that are admitted to the Herb-garden are few. We need only speak of four. They are Chives, *Allium Schœnoprasum ;* Squills, *Urginea maritima ; Crocus vernus*, the True Saffron, also known as *Crocus sativus ;* and *Colchicum autumnale*, the Meadow Saffron, or Autumn Crocus.

Once we have grown *Chives*, we shall never like to be without them. The dainty little bulbs are never eaten, but only the green spikes that shoot up from them in early spring. They are hollow, like tiny rushes, and do not so much taste of Onion as suggest it. They must be used when fresh, and the great delicacy of their flavour makes them invaluable in fastidious cookery. Sydney Smith said of the Onion that 'scarce suspected it should animate the whole.' He would have appreciated Chives. The Hon. Mrs. Evelyn Cecil, in her *History of Gardening*, tells us that they are mentioned in a list of Herbs at the beginning of a cookery book of the fifteenth century; but for the last hundred years they have been out of fashion. This is really a loss to the English public. Anyone wishing to make a sandwich that is sure to be liked has only to put a few of the green spikes of Chives between thin slices of bread and butter. Nothing could be more wholesome, tonic, or enjoyable.

The flowers are blue and the plant altogether attractive; there is a quaintness about it which makes it look at home among the Herbs. Chives can be propagated by division. When the leaves, or rather spikes, are wanted for use, they should be cut close to the ground, when they will soon spring up again.

Squills, that charming wild-flower which looks so lovely in spring-time on the steep and wind-

blown coasts of Cornwall, grows quite contentedly
either in the Herb or any other garden.   It is the
bulb that furnishes the medicine with which most
of us are familiar.   People generally enjoy the
pretty colour of the blossoms, and forget to be
grateful to the plant for its physic.

The *Saffron Crocus, Crocus sativus*, in the Herb-
borders of modern days may be allowed a place
merely on sufferance, but the old Herbalists held
it in the highest esteem.   We find it mentioned in
Tusser's list of 'Seeds and Herbs for the Kitchen.'
He wrote in the year 1557.

This True Saffron is a native of the East, but
has been cultivated in Great Britain ever since
King Edward III.'s time.   Saffron Hill, Holborn,
was once a garden full of these useful flowers.
It is said that a pilgrim brought the plant to
England, concealed in a hollow staff and at the
peril of his life.   He planted it at Saffron Walden,
in Essex, whence the place derived its name.   The
city arms of Walden bears three Saffron plants, as
given by a charter of Edward VI.   Saffron used to
be presented in silver cups by the Corporation to
some of our sovereigns who visited Walden for the
ceremony.   Five guineas were paid for the pound of
Saffron which was purchased for Queen Elizabeth,

and to constitute this quantity forty thousand flowers were required. Growing Saffron was a lucrative industry. Bulbs, flowers, and seeds were all of value for making into tinctures and syrups. From the flowers are taken the familiar orange-red filaments we buy in a dried state for household use; they are really the anthers of the flower, which protrude beyond the blossom and have given the plant its name, *Crocus*, being derived from a Greek word signifying a thread. Sometimes the stigmata of Marigold are used to adulterate the True Saffron. The flower of *Crocus sativus* is violet, variously striped with deeper or lighter tints, and it is fragrant.

'I must have Saffron to colour the warden pies,' said the clown to Perdita, who was making pasties for the sheep-shearing, and the same sweet colouring matter enriches the cakes and buns of the present day. We use it, too, in starch for colouring lace and linen; but we do not expect it to cure measles, nor do we stuff pillows and cushions with it with a view to its animating and restorative qualities. Nowadays, if one is in a merry mood, none of his friends would say of him, 'He has slept in a sack of Saffron.'

As children, when it was the fashion to keep

canary-birds, how many a pinch of saffron—most
fascinating to play with—would be begged for, to
put in their drinking-water ! We were confident
it would not only improve the colour of their
feathers, but would also give our dickies vigour
and strength while moulting. The dye is such a
lovely rich shade, and colours the water at once.
It will dye the hair, too, magnificently. King
Henry the Eighth forbade its use for this purpose.
In Ireland women sometimes wash their sheets in
Saffron-water, thinking to strengthen their limbs.

Nobody has ever praised Saffron more warmly
than Sir Francis Bacon. ' Saffron conveys medicine
to the heart,' he said, ' cures its palpitation,
removes melancholy and uneasiness, revives the
brain, renders the mind cheerful, and generates
boldness.' Another remark of his was that ' What
made the English people sprightly was the liberal
use of Saffron in their broths and sweetmeats.'

Colchicum autumnale grows wild in English
meadows, particularly in the Midlands. It is
rather a pity that it should be commonly called
Meadow Saffron, for, in spite of its name, it really
has nothing to do with Saffron, and this is apt to
be confusing. Nor is it a Crocus, though it looks
like one ; botanically speaking, it is a Lily. Some-

times it is spoken of as ' Upstart,' for the flower rises bare from the earth in the autumn, and the leaves do not appear till the following spring. The bulb provides the well-known medicine called Colchicum.   This is very powerful, and no un- skilled person should meddle with it.   Colchicum as a physic for rheumatism and for gout has long been known both in England and France.   James the First was prescribed the remedy by a then famous physician, Sir Theodore Mayerne, who mixed it with the powder of unburied skulls.

In the year 1563 persons who were using Colchicum were warned by Turner that ' much of it is sterke poyson, and will strongell a man and kill him in the space of one day.'   The peasantry of France call the bulbs *Tue chien,* or *Morte aux chiens,* which shows they are aware of their dan- gerous qualities.   The bulbs are taken up in the spring.   The colour of the flower is a light purple, often more or less mottled.

Like most other bulbous plants, all those we have mentioned like a sandy soil and perfect drainage.   A sandy loam suits them very well.

COMMON SAGE IN FLOWER

(Page 99)

GATHERING, DRYING, AND STORÍNG

CHAPTER X

GATHERING, DRYING, AND STORING

' Doing things in good time is the main secret of successful gardening.'

' We'll make the Mint's remembered spices serve us
For autumn as in spring.'

WE have now completed what we had to say about kitchen Herbs, so it is a good place to speak of their drying and storage.

They must be gathered on a fine dry day, just when they are in the pink of condition, and we had better be ready beforehand with a suitable place in which to dry them. This should be both shady and airy.

We should also be provided with labels, ready written, trays, hooks, string, paper, etc. Care must be taken to prevent the Herbs from getting dusty, and to keep each kind separate.

Just before they flower is a good time for cutting, except when flower-heads are wanted, as

99

with Camomile and Lavender; these should be cut just before the flowers are open.

Advice given by the oldest of our Herbalists and that of the most modern are in absolute agreement.   Both shall be given.

To begin with the oldest: 'Gather Herbs when the sap is full in the top of them.   Such Herbs as you intend to gather for drying, to keep for use all the winter, do it about Lammas-tide; dry them in the shade that the sun draw not out their vertue, but in a clear air and breezy wind, that no mustiness may taint them.'

The following is the counsel given in the Summer Catalogue of one of our leading florists:

'The Basils, Marjorams, Sage, Savorys, and Thyme are in constant demand for drying.   The proper time to gather herbs is just when they are mature.   They must be dried in the shade, and should then be loosely placed in paper bags (labelled) for use during winter.'

We agree with the above except about the paper bags.   We find that once the Herbs are dry enough to crumble it is better to pour them into wide-necked bottles, which should be securely corked.   They keep better in this way than in bags, look neater, and are more handy for the cook. I am sorry **not to** be able to give advice about blending the different Herbs for certain dishes. This used to be done, I know, and perhaps some old cookery-books may treat of the matter.

Mint should be dried and stored, in addition to the Herbs mentioned above; it is so constantly called for in the kitchen. Mint-leaves, dried and candied, too, are excellent. At Grasse they take their place with the candied Violets and Rose-leaves and Orange-flowers prepared in the manufacturies of dried fruits and flowers for eating.

Parsley cannot be dried for use like other Herbs, but can be made brittle by being placed in a tin roasting-screen close to a large fire, when it should be rubbed fine and put away for store.

Whether we dry and keep Camomile-flowers, Marigold-petals, Caraway and Coriander seeds, and a good many other things, is a matter of taste. Lavender-flowers, of course, we save, but not for the kitchen. We ourselves take quite a pride in making cakes and buns flavoured with home-grown Caraway seeds. Perhaps it is only fancy that makes us think them particularly sweet and nice.

All the winter the dried Herbs are a great joy to us, the different flavours remaining so fresh that one would think the garden was still providing them; and so, indeed, it often does right into November, for after being cut back, the plants make fresh growth, so that there are several harvests of the same plant. As winter approaches, it is good to see all the useful perennial inhabitants of the Herb-garden well prepared against rough weather by having made close, sturdy growth. Thus they will get but little harm from winter winds and frost.

Our July Herb-harvest is quite a gala time. The different greens and greys of the leaves look charming as the baskets are filled and taken away for drying. Bunches of them tied up and sent to friends are always welcome, since we have many kinds that cannot be bought in shops. Few of us, I imagine, unless we happen to be vegetarians, would be content with a dinner of Herbs, whether or not love accompanies it; but certainly not even the stalled ox will give us a good dinner without them.

> ' Lord, I confess, too, when I dine,
> The pulse is Thine,
> And all those other bits that be
> There placed by Thee:
> The Wurts, the Perslane, and the mess
> Of Watercress.'

COLOUR IN THE HERB-GARDEN

THE CRIMSON BERGAMOT

One of the most brilliantly coloured herbs.   Its old
name is Bee-Balm

CHAPTER XI

' Farewell, dear flowers ; sweetly your time ye spent,
Fit while ye lived for smell or ornament,
    And after death for cures.'

WHAT is a Herb ? I have always thought Lady
Rosalind Northcote's definition a good one :
' Speaking generally, a Herb is a plant, green and
aromatic, and fit to eat; but it is impossible to
deny that there are several undoubted Herbs that
are not aromatic—a few more grey than green, and
one or two unpalatable, if not unwholesome.'
Gerarde's *Herbal* was divided into three books:
The first treated of ' Grasses, Rushes, Corn, Flags,
Bulbous or Onion-rooted plants'; the second of
' all sorts of Herbes for meat, medicine, or sweete-
smelling use '; the third ' hath trees, shrubs, bushes,
fruit-bearing plants—Rosins, Gums, Roses, Heath
Mosses, Mushrooms, Corall, and their several

kindes.' It is impossible to define 'Herb' exactly, for, like many other words in the English language, the meaning of the word 'Herb' has changed.

The word, however, has gained as well as lost. Though now used in a more restricted sense than formerly—I mean in Bible times, as well as times much later—it has come, has it not, to possess a kind of glamour? 'There is something in the word herb almost as charming and poetic as there is in the word flower. It means to most of us something old - fashioned and sweet - scented and charming, quite as much as something useful.' These words, caught sight of the other day in a book not written for gardeners, expresses exactly the idea.

It is difficult to see how the line between Herbs and other plants can be drawn quite in the way suggested by Gerarde, because so many flowering things, besides being beautiful and sweetly scented, are also good for meat and medicine, like Roses, Violets, and Lilies. There is, however, an un-written law. We seem to know by instinct what plants belong to the Herb-border, in addition to those that have a natural right there, like the kitchen, confectionery, and medicinal Herbs.

Those who wish to have brilliant colours in their

borders may be glad of the following list of plants
that generally have a ticket of admittance to the
Herb-garden. Every one of them is good for smell
or cure, as well as for ornament. They are:
Valerian, *Valeriana officinalis;* Hyssop, *Hyssopus
officinalis;* Mallows, *Malva;* Chicory, *Cichorium;*
Bergamot, *Monarda;* Sweet Woodruff, *Asperula
odorata,* a perennial; and the little Blue Woodruff,
which is an annual. Besides these Herbs with gay
flowers, we have already spoken of the brightness
in the Herb-border of Marigold, Borage, and Cat-
Mint.

Valerian is a plant whose white or crimson
flowers would be attractive anywhere, and everybody knows its value as a physic. The Spikenard
of Scripture is made from a Valerian that grows
in the Himalayan Ranges. Cats delight in the
Valerian of our gardens. Occasionally my Persian
cat goes wild over it, gnawing at the roots like any
savage, though as a rule he is the best behaved
cat in the kingdom.

Hyssop is a handsome evergreen shrub, with
purple-blue or mauve flowers, which, if not exactly
gay, are lively-looking enough to have a footing
in some flower-gardens. Along with Cat-Mint,
Hyssop makes a charming border, their soft in-

distinct blues going well together. It was Miss Jekyll, I think, who first introduced Cat-Mint and Hyssop into our flower-gardens. There is one garden of her designing I know very well where two broad beds on either side a broad gravel walk are planted entirely with these two Herbs, whose gentle hues blend admirably. At the back of the borders bushes of Rosemary and Lavender are planted ; a grey stone wall and comfortable wooden bench complete the scene, which is full of repose, and good for heart and eyes.

We are sorry we cannot claim for our Hyssop that it is the Hyssop of the Bible ; about that, however, there is much discussion. Formerly it was a sacred Herb and chosen for cleansing sacred places. In the accounts we were reading this very year of the consecration of the Westminster Cathedral the use of Hyssop was mentioned in the 'sprinkling of the altars.' How curious and interesting is this continuance of a ceremonial so ancient !

As a kitchen Herb, Hyssop was used more for broths and decoctions than for salads. The flowers, like those of the Cat-Mint, go on blooming all the summer through, which makes the plants an ornament from June to October.

Mallows are as good as they are pretty. Their very name comes from a word that means to soften. Who does not know the French *Pâtes-de-Gimauve?* They are made from the root of the Marsh Mallow. The leaves and sap are also full of virtue. Their curious round seeds are called by schoolboys bread and cheese, and a poet has written of fairy chariots drawn by mice with

> ' Wheels at hand of Mallow-seeds,
>   Which childish sport had strung as beads.'

Several kinds of Mallow may have a place in the Herb - garden. Four varieties, all of which are used medicinally, are represented in our illustration. They are the Common Mallow, *Malva sylvestris*, and the White Mallow; also the large pink and small pink Mallow. The Marsh Mallow, *Althœa officinalis*, is one of the ingredients for the homely *Tisane de quatre fleurs*, which is surely the pleasantest remedy for colds that ever was. A French lady of my acquaintance often mixes it for her family. It is made of Borage, Marsh Mallow, Violet, and the Wild Poppy.

Chicory gives us flowers that may lay claim to providing a tint of the clearest, purest, most stainless blue that can be found anywhere out of God's blue sky. If the blossoms did not grow in such an awkward fashion on their stems, how invaluable they would be for decoration! We know of a man who, while out otter-hunting one day, saw some of these flowers on a bank. He had never noticed them before, but was so struck with their beauty that he could not forget them. He brought them into his garden, had them massed, and they became the admiration of all beholders.

Need anyone be reminded of the uses of Chicory? Many people think the mixture of it with coffee makes that beverage more wholesome than when taken by itself. It is the root that is roasted for use. The blossoms of Chicory once ranked among the cordial flowers.

Bergamot provides flowers of crimson and makes a lovely patch of colour in any garden. An old-fashioned name for the plant, Bee-Balm, is enough to prejudice anyone in its favour. Oil of Bergamot is much used in perfumery. In America a tea is made of the aromatic leaves of one kind of Berga-mot; another kind goes into the preparation known to modern doctors as Thymol. When the good old custom prevailed of carrying little posies to church on Sunday mornings, Bergamot, next to Old Man

(Southernwood), was the favourite with old and young.

Sweet Woodruff, with its dainty little white flowers and clustering foliage of bright green, is a plant more often seen in cottage-gardens than the gardens of the rich. People never seem to know where to put it. In the flower-garden it is a little weedy; in the rock-garden it is almost too quick a spreader; but let the pretty creature have its way somewhere, and no one will begrudge the room it takes. Even this innocent little plant has its enemies; there is a tiresome green beetle, something like a tiny Rose-beetle, who will devour it in hot summers if you let him.

Woodruff and Lavender, woven into garlands, were used of old time in the decoration of churches. To bring out the hay-scent of the leaves they must be crushed or dried, but once dry there is no limit to the time they remain sweet. Withered leaves were put with linen and between the pages of books, where the star-shaped whorls lie perfectly flat and as thin as paper; fresh green leaves, bruised, would be laid against cuts and wounds. Wine and cool drinks were made of Woodruff, and many songs have been sung about it, which preserve the memory of old fancies, superstitions, and uses which once prevailed.

'The Woodruff is a bonny flower, her leaves are set like spurs
About her stem, and honeysweet is every flower of hers.
Yet sweetest dried and laid aside in kist with linen white,
Or hung in bunches from the roof for winterly delight.

'The Woodruff is a bonny flower ; we press her into wine,
To make a cordial comfort for sickly folk that pine.
We plant our graves with Woodruff, and still on holy days
Woodruff on country altars gives out her scent for praise.'

A GROUP OF MALLOWS

(Page 109)

FRAGRANCE IN THE HERB-GARDEN

FRAGRANCE IN THE HERB-GARDEN

CHAPTER XII

FRAGRANCE IN THE HERB-GARDEN

' This broth of smells, that feeds and fats my minde.'

' J'ai des bouquets pour tous les goûts;
Venez choisir dans ma corbeille;
De plusieurs les parfums sont doux
De tous, la vertu sans pareille.'

CONSIDERING how large a part the visible plays in our enjoyment of gardens, it is not a little surprising to notice how much of their charm also depends upon the invisible. Grace of movement, as the wind sways and the sun flickers, and glory of colour, as the flowers come into bloom, are so associated in our minds with the delight of gardens that we forget to recognize the part that is played in them by that which we see not. But is there not something almost more wonderful and subtle about the unseen gift of fragrance than about the more striking gift of colour? Scent is less explainable, less definable, and its wonders have been less explored. There are few better places for the study of scents than the Herb-garden.

Here fragrance depends more on the leaves of plants than on the flowers. One secret is soon discovered. It is the value of leaf-scents. Flower-scents are evanescent; leaf-odours are permanent.

On the other hand, leaf-odours, though ' ready when sought,' do not force themselves upon us, as it were, like flower-scents, which we must smell whether we will or no. Leaf-scents have to be coaxed out by touching, bruising, or pressing ; but there they are. After all, that is the great point, and long after the summer flower-scents have departed we can enjoy the perfumes of the sweet-leaved Herbs and plants, such as Rosemary, Bay, and Thyme. Even when withered, in the depth of winter, how full of fragrance are the natural Herb-gardens of the South of Europe, where one walks over stretches of dry Thyme and Lavender, every step crushing out their sweetness.

Bushy Herbs that are invaluable for the permanence of their leaf-odours are Rosemary, *Rosmarinus officinalis;* Lavender, *Lavandula vera;* Southernwood, *Artemisia abrotanum;* Balm, *Melissa officinalis; Santolina*, also known as French Lavender, or Lavender Cotton ; and the Sweet Bay, *Laurus nobilis.* This last, we confess, is not a Herb, according to the modern meaning of the word ; but, for the sweetness of its leaves, we think a bush or tree of it should be found not far away from any Herb-garden.

Rosemary, so long beloved by English people that some say it was here before the Norman Conquest, was valued for such a number of different reasons that in early times every wise matron and good manager took care to have it in her garden. There may have been some sense in the old saying : ' Where Rosemary flourishes the woman rules.' Rosemary is a plant that wants a little looking after. It came originally from the southern sea-board, and will not grow just anywhere. It likes a well-drained, somewhat sandy soil, and is never happier than when trained close to a wall, or allowed to throw its long wands over sunny stones, where in winter's dearth of outdoor green the lovely colour of its foliage, green lined with silver, is truly welcome.

And why was Rosemary so greatly in request ? It was wanted to make wine, to make physic, to make scent, and is still one of the ingredients of *eau-de-Cologne.* It was stuck into rounds of beef,

and used to season poultry.   Sprigs of it, gilded or
bound with ribbons, were distributed at weddings,
and branches of it would be thrown into graves, as
they were into that of the hapless Ophelia.

> ' Dry up your tears and stick your **Rosemary**
> On this fair corse.'

It was a pretty custom for bridesmaids to present
a bridegroom with a bunch of Rosemary at his
first appearance on his wedding morn.   Rosemary
was an emblem of love and loyalty, so he was to
carry the green sprays in his hand while the warm
feelings they represented were glowing in his heart.
Bees greatly love the flowers of Rosemary.   Sir
Thomas More wrote of it : ' As for Rosmarine, I
let it runne all over my garden walls not onlie
because my bees love it, but because it is the herb
sacred to remembrance and therefore to friendship ;
whence a sprig of it hath a dumb language.'   A
legend of the Rosemary, not so well known as
some, tells how the plant came by its blue flowers.
The Blessed Virgin threw her linen over a white-
flowered shrub to bleach it ; ever afterwards the
flowers were as blue as the Virgin's robe.

Rosemary is best grown from cuttings, which
may be planted in August, either in the open or in
light loam in boxes, kept under cover during the

winter. The following April they can be bedded out. In a chalky soil Rosemary is said to grow smaller, but to be more fragrant and hardy. We grow ours from cuttings, put in against some sheltered wall, where they do very well.

' *Lavender, sweet Lavender !*' Do we not all know Lavender by heart, and love its spikes of azure bloom ? It is one of the Herbs we must grow generously. It is so pleasant to be able to gather as many of its sprays as we like, to keep and dry for our own use or to give away. Many a poet has sung of Lavender :

> ' Lavender is for lovers true,
> Which ever more be faine,
> Desiring always for to have
> Some pleasure with their paine.'

Tennyson liked to see White Lilies and Sweet Lavender growing together—

> ' Opening upon level plots
> Of crowned Lilies standing near
> Purple spikèd Lavender.'

There are several kinds of Lavender. We may have the broad-leaved or the narrow-leaved ; the latter is considered the hardier. All the different sorts should be grown: the Munstead Early, the Dwarf, and the charming White-flowered, which is as sweet as any and far more uncommon. This requires a little more care than the Blue-flowered, and it is safer to plant it in spring than in autumn. Lavender is not always easy to please; it likes rather a poor, sandy, even stony soil, wide, open spaces, and plenty of sunshine. Loam over chalk also suits it. Two important points to look after are good drainage and entire freedom from damp in winter. We propagate by cuttings, but some adopt the plan of layering. After the third year the Lavender bushes become straggly. Care must be taken always to have young plants ready to follow on. The Dwarf Lavender remains a nice little compact shrub longer than any other, and it has larger blooms, but for sweetness the ordinary Lavenders of our gardens are perhaps the best. They are *Lavandula vera* and *Lavandula spica*.

In Spain there is a Lavender, *L. stœchas*, from which the people of the country extract an oil by the simple process of hanging it, flowers downwards, in a closed bottle in the hot sunshine. They use the oil to dress wounds. Lavender-water is perhaps the cleanest smelling of all refreshing scents, and it is pleasant to know that better Lavender for the market cannot be had anywhere than that produced in our own breezy English Lavender-fields.

Myrtle

Purple Lavender
(*Beyond gate*)

Wormwood

Great Mullein
(*Beyond gate*)

Bergamot

Rue

Sweet Marjoram

Hyssop

White Lavender

Creeping and Common Thyme

FRAGRANCE IN THE HERB-GARDEN

(*Page* 115)

Southernwood, so quaintly nicknamed Old Man or Lad's Love, is a plant more frequently found in cottage than in sophisticated gardens. Why it is called Lad's Love we have often wondered, and have been told that country boys think the ashes of it a good thing to make the hair grow on their faces, and that is why they love it. More likely it is because the younger people are, the more a good strong scent attracts them. Many a young child has learned the alphabet of smelling in our Herb-garden, and there is no plant they enjoy the smell of so much as the strongly scented Southernwood. This is not surprising when we remember that the human race in its infancy enjoyed perfumes of a much heavier kind than would be tolerated in these days.

The smell of Southernwood keeps off moths—so the French say, and call it *Garde-robe*. The scent is too individual to harmonize with any other in a nosegay, yet for some it has great fascination.

> ' I'll give to him
> Who gathers me more sweetness than he'd dream
> Without me, more than any Lily could—
> I, that am flowerless, being Southernwood.'

For the sake of its feathery grey-green foliage, we grow another plant among the Herbs something like Old-Man, only finer, more delicate-looking, and without the refreshing smell. In homely language this plant is Old-Woman; the Latin name for it is *Artemisia maritimum*.

Balm, with its delicious lemon scent, is by common consent one of the most sweetly-smelling of all the Herbs in the garden. We like bushes of it everywhere, so that it is always at hand; and handled it must be before it shows how sweet it is. Balm-wine was made of it, and a tea which is good for feverish colds. The fresh leaves make better tea than the dry. With us the Balm dies down in winter.

Santolina, or French Lavender, sometimes called Lavender-Cotton, has no particular sweetness, but a fairly pleasant, strong, clean scent. The grey foliage makes it valuable as an edging plant. It used to be put in garlands for decoration, and was mixed with other sweet Herbs for strewing.

Sweet Bay, or Poet's Laurel, was so often used along with Rosemary and other Herbs that it seems unfair to exclude it from our list altogether. A branch of Bay: how much that means—victory, joy, triumph! And at one time Bay was regarded as a panacea for every ill. In my childhood we were brought up almost on Bay-trees, for two

famous ones grew in my father's garden. Reiterated
warnings not to chew Bay-leaves 'because of the
prussic acid in them' had the effect of investing
these trees with a weird interest. Every rice-
pudding in which a limp Bay-leaf was innocently
swimming became at once a viand worthy of
respect, and was uplifted altogether above its usual
insipidity.

Nor have we spoken of *Myrtle*, sweet as it is and
in nature so often associated with Herbs. There are
sheltered English gardens where Myrtle will exist,
no doubt, but not very many where it will thrive;
and anyone who has seen how happy it is, still
glossy green in February, among the withered
Thymes and Lavenders of the herbage of sunny
stone-scattered places in the French Riviera, will
never care to plant it where winter cold shrivels its
leaves, making them so brown and sere that it
takes more than a few summer months to recover
its good looks. A flowering Myrtle is one of the
luckiest plants it is possible to have, say the people
of the West Country; and if the leaves crackle in
the hands, that shows the person beloved will prove
faithful. However this may be, 'crackling' them is
one way of bringing out the good smell of the plant,
never very powerful, though so universally liked.

It is pleasant to know that sweet odours are not only harmless, but actually beneficial, and I am convinced that if our London florists were to make more of a feature of providing us with hardy, durable, fragrant foliage, as well as flowers, the public would be glad. They might give us branches of Sweet Bay, Myrtle, Rosemary, Southernwood, and all the sweet-leafed Geraniums, with bunches of Lemon Thyme, and that exquisitely scented Lemon Mint of which I have already spoken. Bunches of green and purple Sage, too, would find many admirers. In a sick-room I have known a nosegay of nothing but Herbs and fragrant leaves give more pleasure than anything. Their way of not giving up their scent unless asked to do so is a positive advantage, as it is impossible for them to become oppressive. A belief that sweet scents are wholesome is very widespread. The Malays stuff their beds and pillows with the fragrant Herb from which patchouli is made, and the name they have given this plant means 'fragrant and healthy.' Eucalyptol has been detected in Rosemary, Sage, and Lavender, and many flower and leaf scents are known to be both antiseptic and germicidal.

Modern research has proved, too, that ozone is

developed when the sun shines on most kinds of
fragrant plants, such as scented flowers, Fir and
Pine trees, and sweet Herbs generally. This idea
makes the hours we spend in a sunny fragrant
garden more delightful than ever.

And not only gardens such as these, but their
harvests, gathered up and garnered, are full of
virtue, which happily they retain. In one of his
essays, Sir William Temple, describing the effects
of a visit he once paid to a storehouse that was
full of many kinds of spicery, declared that he
and his party felt so renewed and revived by the
aromatic fragrances around them as to enjoy for
a long time afterwards 'an exaltation of good
health, good humour, and good spirits.' He was
in agreement with John Evelyn, that wise and
famous gardener of old, who soberly proposed to
make London the healthiest as well as the happiest
city in Christendom, by encompassing it with plots
and hedgerows of Sweetbriar, Jasmine, Lilies,
Rosemary, Musk, and Marjoram. One cannot but
suppose that the gardens at King Edward VII.
Sanatorium at Midhurst were laid out and furnished
according to this idea, such a large number of the
beds and borders being filled with Rosemary,
Lavender, Hyssop, Cat-Mint, Santolina, and many

other wholesome and aromatic plants. Doubtless they exercise a beneficial influence.

Will our doctors ever let scents take a recognized place in modern physics? What we breathe must surely be of quite as great importance to us as what we eat or drink.

WILD HERBS FOR PHYSIC

WILD CHICORY

CHAPTER XIII

WILD HERBS FOR PHYSIC

'In physic by some signature
Nature herself doth point a cure.'

'Somewhere, somewhere grows the Herb of Healing ;
Is it a Herb of the Sea ?'

IF we take the trouble to investigate the history
and the medicinal or mystical properties that
belong to any Herb or flower, we are at once
confronted by a past that is full of fascination.
The present and the past are linked together ; old
facts look at us with young faces.

Much as we may smile at the old Herbalists
for the faith they placed in the healing virtues of
certain of our wildlings, it is nevertheless true
that modern research has justified that faith. We
turn the light of science on it and smile no longer,
for we find that, in spite of its alloy with magic,
astrology, and superstition, much of the solid

gold of truth remains. The old-fashioned Herbal Simples that once were used were really remedies, and instead of laughing at them, we begin to wonder how so much that was true and useful could have been found out.

It was partly done by watching the self-cure of animals. Has anyone ever noticed how at many an old farmstead a goat will be kept as if for luck, and apparently for no other reason? This is a survival from the days when the goat was thought the ' Herbalist Quadruped,' clever in finding Herbs that were good for physic. Early man must often, we imagine, have experimented on himself. Poor Eve with the apple—what a signal failure was her experiment! It was doubtless one of the first. Long afterwards the sons of the prophets gathered gourds and shred them into the pot. These were experimenters and discoverers of a valuable medicine—the Colocynth, or Bitter Apple.

Our wild Herbs are as full of virtue as ever, and we still depend on them for medicine; but the chemist in the laboratory extracts their goodness for us. The gathering and preparing of Herbal Simples for ourselves is a lost art. One is sometimes asked the question, What is the art of ' Simpling '? It consists in curing common ailments with simple single remedies, culled from the soil. The word 'drug' came originally from the Anglo-Saxon verb *drigan*, to dry, as applied to medicinal plants.

In the Midlands and northern parts of England, however, the reign of the Herbalist is not yet over. Workmen in potteries and puddling furnaces have found that a tea made of tonic Herbs is cheaper and less intoxicating than ordinary beer. Other preparations are used for colds and fevers. Not long ago, while staying in the Midlands, we came in for the weekly fair and market-day at an ancient county town. Crockery, furniture, carpets, sweets, live ducks, clothing, and all manner of other things, were set out to tempt the buyer; but what interested us most was the stall of the Herbalist, looking rather grim, with its sign of crossbones and human skull, over which appeared the legend, 'Consult me, if you would not come to this.' A little farther north again, written in very large letters over a very small shop, we found the words, '*Dandelion Stout* sold here at 2d. a bottle.' We thought this very satisfactory. Dandelion is good for eating, too. Did not Betsy Prig's famous salad contain 'a trifle of the Herb called Dandelion'? Country-folk believe that to cure sick sheep you have only to drive them into a field full of Dandelions.

It was also satisfactory to hear that two large wholesale firms in London deal in Herbs for Simples, such as are in use in the rural parts of Northern and Mid-England, and are doing a good trade.

The grandmother of our own gardener was a Herb-woman, and used to perambulate the towns and villages of Norfolk selling her simples. Much of her knowledge is remembered and passed on to the present generation. Would we consent to it, most of our common ailments might be cured for us by weeds or wildlings from our own fields and garden. Meadow Crowfoot is offered for an inflamed eye; House-Leeks from the roofs cure scalds and heal sore places: they were planted there for that very purpose more than sixty years ago, when many a fretful infant found the benefit of their juices, mixed with cream and applied to relieve the discomforts of vaccination. Syrup made from flowers of the Red Clover is a fine remedy in whooping-cough; Cabbage-leaves, put on hot, are prescribed to wrap outside sore throats; leaves of Yarrow will cure headaches or stop nose-bleeding; the juice of any sort of Buglos is softening in chest complaints.   Colt's-foot will cure bronchitis, and Groundsel heal chapped hands.   Eyebright makes dim eyes see; Plantain seeds can be used when we run short of linseed ; and the darling little Pimpernel, or Poor-Man's-Weather-glass—well, I trust we shall not want to use that, for it is a remedy for the bites of mad dogs ; it is also supposed to remove all sadness.   It is curious that the Pimpernel should have won this character for cheerfulness among the English ; a name for it in Greek means to laugh.   Next to the Speedwell, no wild flower in Britain is more beloved than this.

> 'No ear hath heard, no tongue can tell,
>   The virtues of the Pimpernel.'

Betony, a rather pretty wild flower found in woods or shady meadows, was once the sovereign remedy for all maladies of the head.   An old Italian proverb says: 'Sell your coat and buy Betony.'   The chief physician to the Emperor Augustus wrote a whole book on nothing but the merits of this plant, and its very name, from the Celtic *ben*, head, and *tonic*, good, is in its favour ; yet, to tell the truth, modern chemistry fails to discover why it was thought quite so much of. That there is some virtue in the plant seems to be proved, however, by the fact that not so very long ago a snuff was made from its dried leaves by an English Herbalist, and sold to cure nervous headaches. At one time this snuff was quite famous. A mere pinch of the powdered Herb provokes violent sneezing.

In the long list of healing Herbs that spring up about our feet, not one is more interesting or speaks to us more eloquently of past and present than the dear little low-growing Eyebright, *Euphrasia officinalis.* Many of us do not so much as know this plant by sight; but it is common enough on heaths and mountains by the sea, or may sometimes be found, if looked for, among the grasses of our lawns, only these are clipped too closely as a rule for the plant to show its tiny flowers. From the earliest times this weed has been famous for restoring and preserving eyesight. It is the same Herb that the Greeks named after the linnet, because she was the first to discover its power, and passed the knowledge on from birddom to mankind. Culpepper, the old astrologer-physician, declared of the Eyebright that if its uses were generally understood, spectacle-makers would be ruined, and modern chemists are little less complimentary in their remarks.   A tincture made from the whole plant, and mixed with rose-water, is one of the finest eye-lotions that can be made.   Milton, in his ' Paradise Lost,' describes how the angel Michael touched the eyes of Adam with Euphrasie (the Eyebright) and Rue, to give him clearer vision.

The popular names of many of the healing Herbs explain what was believed to be their different characters, such as Clary, or Clear-eyes ; Prunella, or Self-heal; Heart's-ease ; Pulmonaria, or Lungwort ; Woundwort or Bruisewort ; Feverfew ; Gout-weed ; Whitlow-grass, or Nailwort ; Stitch-wort (for a stitch in the side) ; and many others that will occur to any who are familiar with the names of the common plants of the country-side. The acrid Buttercup, the wild Pansy of the field, and the Sundew from the marsh, all had their uses, and would often act in double fashion, either to cause or cure particular ailments.

The doctrine of Signatures, as it was called, was firmly believed in by the old Herbalists.   The idea was that, by the mercy of God, many of the Herbs that He made for the service of man were stamped, as it were, or signed with their characters, so that they could be read at a glance.   Viper's Bugloss,

for instance, had its stems speckled like a snake
or viper, so it cured snake-bites and the stings of
scorpions.   In spite of its pretty Forget-me-not
blue flowers, the plant has a prickly, viperish look,
which makes it very distinctive.   Pulmonaria, or
Lungwort, has broadish leaves, spotted and marked
in a manner which is supposed to resemble the lungs
of men and animals.   The Heart-trefoil has heart-
shaped leaves, which are sometimes blood-stained,
so this Herb protects the heart; the leaves of
St. John's Wort look as if they were perforated
with tiny holes like the pores of the skin, so here
we have a Herb that cures cuts and abrasions; and
(curious indeed) the charming little purple blossom
of the Eyebright is marked with a spot of yellow,
darker in the middle, which has a distinct resem-
blance to a human eye, quite enough to remind
anybody of it.

St. John's Wort deserves a passing mention of
its more than mere medicinal virtues.   It is one
of the most magical of Herbs.   Evil spirits positively shudder at it, flying off at the first whiff
of its scent.   Meg Merrilies knew this when she
sang :

> ' Trefoil, Vervain, John's Wort, Dill,
>   Hinder witches of their will.'

Many are the legends woven about this plant. To give one of them : The peasants of the Isle of Man declare that if after sunset on St. John's Eve you happen to step on the plant, a fairy horse arises out of the ground, which will carry you gloriously all the night, to leave you, wherever you may happen to be, when the first ray of the rising sun flies over the world. In English villages a salve made of the golden flowers is still much used and valued. We grow a prettier kind of St. John's Wort than the common one. It is *Hypericum uralum.*

One Herb of Healing grows wild with us that might not flourish so well inland ; it is the Sea Tree-Mallow, a tall plant, growing quite five or six feet high. The large green leaves are so exquisitely soft that anyone who touches them in the dark would think that they were velvet ; they are used for sprains, steeped in hot water and laid on the injured part. Another Herb of the sea is the Scurvy-grass, *Cochlearia officinalis,* which before our sailors took to Lime-juice was such a blessing to them. Our great navigators have borne testimony to its unfailing use in scurvy. However far from the sea-coast this plant is found, its taste is always salt ; it is supposed to be the famous *Herba*

18

Britannica of the ancients.   We grow two kinds, the English and the Danish.   They always interest sailors.

Enthusiasts wishing to start a physic-garden can do a great deal towards furnishing it by seeking for themselves the healing Herbs they want.   Perhaps it is easier for us to find the plants than for most, because we are so close to the sea, near which so many of them grow, and not far from the Broads, a fine hunting-ground for the botanist.   Such a physic-garden might, perhaps, be thought more a museum than a practical garden. But why should it not be of practical use some-times?   Remedies are not really better for being done up with chemist's cunning in all the bravery of white paper, scarlet sealing-wax, and pink string. These are attractive, no doubt, and aids to faith (which is half the battle), but supposing customary medicines happened to be out of reach, and there was anybody at hand who understood how to use plain remedies from the garden or field, how pleasant such remedies would be, and how welcome if we only believed in them !

In olden times such a garden formed part of every domain of dignity.   It was generally ' My Lady's Garden,' and my lady had learned the practical uses of all the plants that grew in it; such knowledge was part of her education. As good George Herbert said in 1620 : ' In the knowledge of simples, wherein the manifold wisdom of God is wonderfully to be seen, one thing should be carefully observed, which is, to know what herbs may be used instead of drugs of the same nature, and to make the garden the shop. . . . Accordingly, for salves his wife seeks not the City, but prefers her garden and fields before all outlandish gums. And surely Hyssop, Valerian, Mercury, Adder's-tongue, Yarrow, Melicot and St. John's Wort, made into a salve, and Elder, Camomile, Mallows, Comphrey and Smallage made into a poultice, have done great and rare cures.'

OTHER HERBS OF INTEREST

CHAPTER XIV

OTHER HERBS OF INTEREST

'Madam, wol ye stalk
Pryvely into the garden to see the herbes grow ?
And forth on they wend
Passing forth softly into the herbery.'

BESIDES the wild Herbs just spoken of, there are others that may be cultivated, which are of great interest for different reasons. Here are one or two of the kind we mean :

Liquorice, *Glycyrrhiza glabra ;* Angelica, *Archangelica officinalis ;* Elecampane, *Inula Helenium*, Vervain, *Verbena officinalis ;* Mullein, *Verbascum Thapsus ;* Fumitory, *Fumaria officinalis ;* Samphire, *Crithmum maritimum ;* and the wonderful Mandrake, *Mandragora.*

Liquorice is grown for its usefulness, as everybody knows. The plant is hardy, the flowers are bluish, and the value of the plant lies in the root.

143

You may pull a piece of it up, and the taste will soon show what it is.

Angelica and *Elecampane* make excellent sweet-meats. The former is a stately plant about four to six feet in height, stem and leaves covered with a plum-like bloom. Naturally it loves to grow by running water, but puts up with ordinary garden soil quite happily. Seeds of Angelica should be sown as soon as ripe. If the seed is not saved, the plant may be cut down in May, and the stock will send out side-shoots ; by repeating the process the same plant may be long continued. Angelica is a great ornament to the garden, and it is really interesting to cut a hollow stalk of it, trim it a little, and behold a sweet green stick of Angelica, such as is usually met with in ice-puddings.

Elecampane grows into a tall, stout, downy plant, with very large leaves and bright yellow flowers, something like Sunflowers. The candy that is made of it is quite out of fashion now, yet, besides being of a pleasant taste, it is good for asthma, and some of the properties of Elecampane are said to be highly antagonistic to consumption. Several pretty fables account for its Latin name, *Helenium*. One is that Helen's hands were full of it when Paris carried her away ; another, that it sprang from

LEAVES OF SWEET CICELY (MYRRHIS)
(With bipinnate or fern-like leaves)

ALECOST, OR COSTMARY
With which beer and negus were at one time
flavoured

Helen's tears. In our Herb-garden this last summer some plants of Elecampane growing close to the bright blue blossoms of Alkanet, and not far from a patch of crimson Bergamot, made a lovely splash of colour, set off to advantage by a generous drift behind them of feathery grey-green Wormwood. Our illustration, ' Herbs by the Waterside,' shows Elecampane in blossom very well, only there it is growing along with a flowering blue Sea-holly, which some may deem out of place in the Herb-border ; we admit it on the strength of the roots being good for food, and because the Sea-holly is one of the useful wild plants of Great Britain.

Mullein possesses the same good character for its medicinal qualities as Elecampane, so much so that in Ireland it is cultivated in gardens to supply the local chemists. It is the leaves that are used, boiled in milk, which is strained, then drunk while warm. The tall plant, with its spikes of yellow flowers and large flannel-like leaves, is handsome. Roman ladies who loved golden locks tinged their tresses with a hair-wash made of the flowers. Mullein oil is known to be a valuable destroyer of disease germs.

Vervain is not much of a plant to look at, but as the parent of our delightful garden Verbenas must

19

be regarded with respect. It grows wild in the stoniest places, and for its many virtues was once called the 'Simpler's Joy.' Its juice cured the plague, and as to its magic, to that there is no end. It was a sacred Herb and worn as an amulet. When gathered for this purpose, 'firste they crosse the herbe with their hand, and then they blesse it.'

'Hallowed be thou, Vervein,
    As thou growest on the ground,
For in the Mount of Calvary,
    There thou was first found.'

Fumitory is such a pretty weed that many people cannot bear to pull it up. Its rose-coloured flowers, with little dark purple heads, look something like dressed-up dollies, and children in many parts of Kent speak of the weed affectionately by the name of 'Wax-Dolls.' Why is it called Fumitory? Some say because, when burned, the smoke was used in sorcery. Others have it that, instead of growing from seed, it is produced from vapours rising from the earth. The yellow - flowered Fumitory is even prettier than the purple, and the way in which it spreads about, covering large bare spaces with lightning rapidity, makes one understand why it is called 'Earth-smoke.' No wonder it spreads quickly : the seed-pods burst

as soon as ripe, scattering their tiny artillery in
all directions. On a fine, dry summer morning
it is quite amusing to listen to the constant popping
and cracking. Rustic maidens make a face-wash of
Fumitory—

> ' Whose red and purpled mottled flowers
>   Are cropped by maids in weeding hours,
> To boil in water, milk or whey,
>   For washes on a holiday ;
> To make their beauty fair and sleek,
>   And scare the tan from summer's cheek.'

Fumitory wants no cultivating, but rather repres-
sion. Another name for it is Corydalis.

The *Mandrake* is a gruesome Herb. We live in
hopes of possessing it one of these days, but only
know for certain of two plants of it in England :
one is at Kew Gardens, the other in the Old
Physic Garden, Chelsea. The root is the wonderful part ; it is forked, and has a fanciful resem-
blance to a man. Women of the East placed
great faith in it. ' Give me, I pray thee, of thy
son's Mandrakes,' said the childless Rachel to her
sister Leah. When torn from the earth by its
roots, the Herb was said to utter a shriek, which
none might hear and live. So greatly was the
Mandrake dreaded that, according to old legends,

the only safe way to uproot it was to harness a dog to the plant and let him drag at it. The dog immediately died!

After this it is refreshing to speak of the *Samphire*, suggesting, as it does, the open coast and the salt clean breath of the sea. The Samphire flowers are yellow, blooming late in the summer, and leaving little brown ghosts of themselves after fading. The glaucous foliage is full of aromatic juice, and the young shoots, for eating while fresh, or pickling, are gathered in the month of May. Perilous is the harvest, for the plant grows usually in crags and crevices of the most precipitous rocks. Many a life must have been sacrificed to the search for it in the days when Samphire was cried in the London streets as 'Crest Marine'; and Gerarde said of it: 'Samphire is the pleasantest sauce, most familiar and best agreeing with man's body.' Very likely Shakespeare ate Samphire with his dinner the very day he wrote the lovely lines about the sort of place where Samphire grows:

'The crows and choughs that wing the midway air,
Show scarce so gross as beetles; halfway down
Hangs one who gathers Samphire, dreadful trade!
Methinks he seems no bigger than his head:

The fishermen, that walk upon the beach,
Appear like mice . . . the murmuring surge,
That on the unnumbered pebbles chafes,
Cannot be heard so high.'

That is one of the delights of the Herb-garden—
the way it has of taking us back to old-time ways
and doings, recalling them with strange vividness,
much as the simple words of a song we hear recall
the music that belongs to it. Our Samphire plant
is growing among the outside stones of a Herb-
border, and though it came from cliffs on the
warmer side of the Silver Streak, has settled down
with us, and so far is thriving.

The origin of the name Samphire is easy to
trace. Anciently the Herb was known in France
as *Perce-pierre* or *Passe-pierre*. Peter signifying
a rock, the transition to Saint-Pierre was simple,
and the word Samphire we now use in England
resembles the old French form sufficiently to
remind us of it. For centuries the Herb has been
dedicated to St. Peter. In Italy it was *Erba di
San Pietro.*

Some may like to grow Pepperwort (Dittander),
or Poor Man's Pepper, once cultivated in gardens,
and growing wild in some parts of England; or
Fenugreek, a Herb greatly enjoyed by cattle; or

Herb-Patience, also called Monk's Rhubarb ; or Good - King - Henry, otherwise known as Shoemaker's Heels ; or Smallage, a kind of wild celery ; or Cardoons, a sort of Artichoke ; or Lang-de-Beefe and Lovage, the tops of which were eaten. Many of these forgotten Herbs were valued at a time when modern vegetables were unknown.

Nothing would be easier than to add long lists of plants which might go into the Herb-garden ; but what we put into it is really a matter for individual choice. Some like to fill their garden with curiosities ; some are mostly concerned in making it as beautiful as possible ; others think that a Herb-garden should be kept entirely for such things as strike the eye at once as Herbs. No two people would furnish their Herb-garden alike. Let each one please himself. One of the best things about gardening is its infinite variety.

WHAT MODERN WRITERS ARE SAYING ABOUT HERBS AND HERB-GARDENS

CHAPTER XV

WHAT MODERN WRITERS ARE SAYING ABOUT
HERBS AND HERB-GARDENS

'In the multitude of counsellors there is wisdom.'

'Excellent Herbs had our fathers of old,
   Excellent Herbs to ease their pain ;
Alexanders and Marigold,
   Eyebright, Orris, and Elecampane,
Basil, Rocket, Valerian, Rue
   (Almost singing themselves they run),
Vervain, Dittany, Call-me-to-you,
   Cowslip, Melilot, Rose of the Sun.'

Rewards and Fairies.

WE have quoted a good deal of what the old writers had to say about Herbs, for it is almost impossible to avoid being somewhat carried away by the fascination of that part of the subject ; but it occurs to us that it may be helpful to our readers if we collect and give them the benefit of what some of our best modern gardeners have been writing lately on the same topic. To match the extreme modernity of this chapter, we have even secured some lines of an up-to-date poet, whose verses, written just in time, have as true a ring as if they were a hundred years old.

In the course of last July, while we were in the midst of enjoying the aromatic pleasures of our garden of Herbs, then greatly in perfection, we were pleased to notice in the pages of a well-known weekly periodical* a pleasant and useful column devoted entirely to the subject of culinary Herbs and their cultivation. We have the author's permission to quote it, and are entirely in sympathy with what is said, especially in the idea of using Parsley as an edging plant; it is what we frequently do ourselves, thereby imitating the Greek gardeners of old, who had such a habit of bordering their gardens with Parsley and Rue that a saying arose when an undertaking was contemplated, but not yet commenced, 'Oh, we are only at the Parsley and Rue.'

'A garden of herbs—there is savouriness in the very name. And yet often the most unsatisfactory things in gardens, especially small ones, are the herbs. Scattered here and there all over the place, they have mostly a ragged, neglected look, and are

* Donald McDonald in *The Queen* for July 30, 1910.

very often not to be found when wanted; and if they are, time and patience are probably exhausted in hunting them up when wanted in a hurry for flavouring. Quite a pleasing feature might be made in even a small garden of the herbs were they only brought together and arranged in order. The best position for herbs is in beds, and these may be made from two or four feet wide, with foot alleys between them, and the length at the least one-third more than the width. This disposition in beds is so much more convenient and better in appearance than rows at regular intervals, which remind one more of herb-growing for medicines or perfumes, not of gatherings and snippings for culinary purposes. In small gardens one entire bed will not be needed for any one herb, and in them several may be grown together in one bed, such for instance, as common and lemon thyme, pennyroyal, and marjoram in one; fennel, sage, and tarragon in another; and basil, summer savory, and golden purslane together. Mint should have a bed to itself, as mint sauce is always in demand, and almost everyone likes it with lamb and for flavouring peas. Chervil, too, is often required for salads. Some may also desire to reserve a bed for angelica, for the luxury of its young shoots candied in sugar, and the growth of borage, for the flavouring of claret-cups.

'Again, the herb-garden is just the place for the systematic cultivation of small salading, such as a succession of young onions, a bed of chives, radishes, rampion, lettuce, endive. All these would furnish a good many beds, and by changing those that are not permanent for different products, a nice succession of cropping might be maintained. A parsley-bed or beds must not be omitted, for nothing is more useful in a household, alike for flavouring or garnishing, and it is just as easy on a right system to have fine leaves, exquisitely curled and clean, because raised high above the ground by their strength of stature, as to have and use the small dirty leaves that have to do duty as parsley in many households. Let the parsley have a bed of rich, deep soil ; sow the best curled seed thinly ; as soon as up thin the plants to six inches apart, and then let them grow away freely. That is the whole art of growing and using parsley, and making it one of the finest foliaged plants in the garden. Sow in July for succession. If the garden of herbs is too small for the devotion of one or more beds to parsley sown at different seasons, then the whole herb-garden might be fringed round with it, and the flowering plants themselves be garnished with its beauty.

'Sage is **one of** the most useful **of** garden herbs, and may be grown from either seeds **or cuttings.** Spring is the usual season for sowing the seeds, although they can be put in **now** in a shady spot and firm soil. Cuttings may also be taken out now, choosing those shoots that **do not** show a flower head at the **top** ; they will root steadily in a fairly moist soil, and unless the sun is very bright will not need any shading. I have seen gardeners put a spadeful or two of earth into the heart **of** a sage-bush, and the growths thus covered soon **take** root ; they are then separated from the old bush and planted alone. Thyme—both common and lemon—is another herb much in request **for** culinary requirements. It may be raised from seeds or cuttings or by dividing the plant. **An** open position is essential, as full exposure **to** the air increases the aromatic properties, much of which is lost when the plant is smothered up with other things. For keeping purposes thyme should be **cut** when at the height of its flowering.

'Of mint several varieties are grown, but the spear-mint is the most useful. Mint does not produce seeds in **our** climate, but is easily increased by

cuttings made of pieces of the creeping underground
stems, which grow freely when supplied with plenty
of moisture. During summer, when the stems are
full of juice, is the best time to gather mint to dry
for winter use.

' No portion of a garden, large or small, will afford
more pleasure than the herb-garden when it is well
kept and furnished. There will always be something growing and doing in it, and when divided in
the manner stated the different parts are so easily
managed that a bed may be dug or sown at any
spare moment.'

It was interesting to us to find the author advising long narrow beds for growing some of the Herbs
together. As will be seen in our illustration, ' Herb-
Borders in Spring,' this is very much what we have
done. He also gives the same advice as we do
about the advisability of a special bed for Spear or
Lamb Mint. His remarks on the fine stature to
which Parsley may attain, if properly treated, are
most true. To see this plant at its very best, grow
it from one seed only, in rich soil ; then you will
find what a handsome plant it makes.

No doubt many of our readers have enjoyed
Mr. H. H. Thomas's last book, *The Ideal Garden.*
In the chapter on ' Garden Planning,' speaking of

terraces and the best ways of using and planting them, he concludes one paragraph by saying, ‘The terrace might lead at one end to a little paved garden and at the other to a garden of herbs.’ We were glad the writer spared a thought in his plans for the oft-neglected Herb-garden. If he meant to give the garden paved walks, that would be delightful in bad weather for the cooks—indeed, for everybody.   Firm, dry walks between the Herb-beds are very necessary ; we can imagine red tiled paths being very comforting and suitable. For ourselves, we cannot boast of paving-stone of any kind, but have fine shingle from the beach, which is a good substitute, as it never holds water nor gets sloppy, as indifferent gravel does.

In Mrs. Davidson’s last book, *Gardens Past and Present*, one chapter is devoted to ‘The Garden of Herbs,’ but in it she tells us more about out-of-the-way, old-fashioned vegetables than anything else, for, as she truly remarks, ‘ the synonym for a kitchen-garden in olden days was the herb-garden.’ A little farther on we read : ‘ Herbs in our modern acceptance of the term are too much neglected nowadays, and an interesting collection might be made, which would always be an attractive corner of a kitchen-garden to those who like to recall old – time associations.' To us this seems like putting the case rather mildly.

Lastly, we will quote a few words from Miss Gertrude Jekyll's latest volume, *Children and Gardens*. Knowing how greatly this writer loves Herbs and aromatic plants in general, we were not surprised to find her advising the children for whom she writes to have a Herb-patch in their little gardens. Tarragon and Chives are among the kinds that are recommended. ' Chives,' she writes, ' is a sort of small onion ; it is planted in tufts. You could have a row of tufts (this is how we plant Chives) or a bit in your kitchen-garden ; it is often grown like this in cottage-gardens.'

It seems to be agreed that the growing of Herbs has been neglected for many a long year. Is there going to be a revival now ? Signs of this are not wanting.

PRACTICAL NOTES FOR REFERENCE

PRACTICAL NOTES FOR REFERENCE

PERENNIAL HERBS.

POPULAR NAME.	BOTANICAL NAME.	TIME TO PLANT.	REMARKS.
Alecost, or Costmary.	Pyrethrum. Tanacetum (Balsamita vulgaris).	Late October or November.	Very old-fashioned ; formerly an ingredient in beer and negus and was used as a strewing Herb
Alkanet, or Bugloss.	Anchusa officinalis.	,,	Has bright blue flowers. Roots formerly used to colour confectionery red ; still used as a dye. Makes excellent rouge
Angelica.	Archangelica officinalis.	,,	Tall, handsome plant ; white flowers. Stalks candied for sweetmeats.
Balm.	Melissa officinalis.	,,	Grown for its fragrant leaves. Balm-tea taken hot is good for colds.
Bergamot, or Beebalm.	Monarda fistulosa.	,,	Has bright flowers, generally crimson. Beloved by bees.
Burnet (salad).	Poterium Sanguisorba.	,,	Out of date now. Once used in salads.
Camomile.	Anthemis nobilis.	,,	A wholesome stomachic is made of the small white flowers.
Cat-mint.	Nepeta cataria.	,,	A spreading blue-flowered plant ; grows anywhere, but best on rockeries in sunshine.
Chicory.	Cichorium Intybus.	,,	Chicory dislikes moving ; does best grown from seed.
Chives.	Allium Schœnoprasum.	,,	The leaves (like hollow blades) taste delicately of onion. The bulbs should not be eaten, though they are sometimes cooked with beef-steaks to season them.
Elecampane.	Inula Helenium.	,,	Tall, handsome plant, with yellow flowers ; once made a popular sweetmeat. Good for coughs and asthma.

163

PERENNIAL HERBS—*continued.*

	BOTANICAL NAME.	TIME TO PLANT.	REMARKS.
Fennel.	*Fœniculum vulgare.*	Late October or November.	Eaten with boiled mackerel; still decorates London fish shops.
Fumitory, or Corydalis.	*Fumaria officinalis.*	,,	A rapid spreader; grows any-where. Flowers yellow, or pinky-purple.
Horehound.	*Marrubium vulgare.*	,,	A wholesome bitter; still used to make beer in some parts of England.
Hyssop.	*Hyssopus officinalis.*	,,	Bears pretty blue flowers; a sacred plant of old; used for cleansing and for physic.
Lavender.	*Lavandula.*	March or April.	A well-known sweet-smelling shrub; used in perfumery and medicine.
Liquorice.	*Glycyrrhiza glabra.*	Late October or November.	A good old-fashioned medicine for coughs and hoarseness.
Lungwort.	*Pulmonaria officinalis*	,,	Has spotted leaves, supposed to resemble the lung and to cure lung diseases.
Mallows.	*Malva.*	,,	All the Mallows are good-look-ing; the least good-looking are the most useful.
Marjoram (pot).	*Origanum Onites.*	,,	One of our best kitchen Herbs; as pretty as it is useful. Must have a large drift of it.
Mints (many varieties have been described).	*Mentha.*	,,	A delightful family. All want plenty of moisture, except Cat-Mint Lamb-Mint should have a good-sized bed to itself, as the cook is always wanting it.
Mullein.	*Verbascum Thapsus.*	,,	Has beautiful soft grey foliage. Golden-yellow flowers. The dried leaves, smoked like tobacco, soothe the most hack-ing cough.
Pennyroyal.	*Mentha pulegium.*	,,	A dwarf Mint, growing close to the ground; flowers very late.
Peppermint.	*Mentha piperita.*	,,	The essential oil of Peppermint owes its virtues to the menthol or mint camphor which it con-tains. A very favourite Mint.
Pepperwort, or Poor Man's Pepper.	*Lepidium latifolium.*	,,	Leaves taste hot; spreads too fast.

PERENNIAL HERBS—*continued*.

POPULAR NAME.	BOTANICAL NAME.	TIME TO PLANT.	REMARKS.
Prunella, or Carpenter's Herb (Self-heal)	*Prunella vulgaris.*	Late October or November.	Corolla shaped like a billhook ; said to heal wounds made by edge-tools.
Rosemary.	*Rosmarinus officinalis.*	,,	A favourite fragrant shrub, doing best by the sea.
Rue.	*Ruta graveolens.*	,,	Cures croup in poultry ; a useful medicine to man and beast.
Saffron.	*Crocus sativus.*	All bulbs should be set in autumn.	A pretty bulbous plant, providing the well-known saffron of commerce.
Sage.	*Salvia officinalis.*	Late October or November.	One of our most useful kitchen Herbs. The purple variety should be grown as well as the green.
St. John's Wort.	*Hypericum perforatum.*	October or November.	A very magical Herb ; heals wounds and cures insanity. Supposed to blossom on St. John's Day.
Samphire.	*Crithmum maritimum.*	Late October or November.	Formerly made a favourite pickle 'of a spicie taste with a certaine saltnesse.' Grows on sea-cliffs.
Santolina, or French Lavender.	*Santolina Chamæcyparissus.*	,,	Has grey-green foliage ; formerly a strewing Herb.
Savory (winter).	*Satureia montana.*	April or October.	Useful in the kitchen.
Sea-holly.	*Eryngium maritimum.*	October or November.	The roots are candied ; they have a sweetish juice.
Sorrel.	*Rumex.*	Any time.	Leaves excellent for flavouring soups. The Sorrels are terrible spreaders.
Southernwood, or Old Man.	*Artemisia Abrotanum.*	,,	An aromatic shrub which never flowers in England. Is liked for its fragrance and cordial qualities.
Sweet Cicely.	*Myrrhis odorata.*	,,	Has fern-like leaves and white flowers. Very attractive to bees.
Tansy.	*Tanacetum vulgare.*	,,	Once used for making puddings at Easter.
Tarragon.	*Artemisia Dracunculus.*	Spring.	A valuable kitchen Herb; makes a famous vinegar.
Thyme.	*Thymus.*	Autumn or Spring. See pp. 59 and 60.	All the Thymes are valuable in cookery or otherwise. Syrup of Common Thyme is a cure for whooping-cough.

PERENNIAL HERBS—*continued*.

POPULAR NAME.	BOTANICAL NAME.	WHEN TO SOW.	REMARKS.
Valerian, or Heal-all.	*Valeriana officinalis.*	Autumn	Bears fine crimson or white flowers. Has powerful medicinal virtues; beloved of cats.
Vervain.	*Verbena officinalis.*	Spring or autumn.	One of the most sacred plants of old; homely in appearance, and has very small flowers.
Woodruff (sweet)	*Asperula odorata*	,,	Leaves hay-scented when dry Infused, they make an exhilarating tea or wine.
Wormwood, or Mugwort.	*Artemisia Absinthium.*	,,	A splendid bitter; used in the preparation of absinthe.

POPULAR NAME.	BOTANICAL NAME.	WHEN TO SOW.	REMARKS.
Anise.	*Pimpinella Anisum.*	If in the open, April, or in a hot bed in March, for setting out in May.	Aniseed tea is an excellent remedy in infantile catarrh. Useful in bronchial complaints.
Basil (sweet green).	*Ocymum Basilicum.*	,,	Interesting spicy little plants; good kitchen herbs, much neglected in England.
Basil (bush green).	*Ocymum minimum.*	,,	
Borage.	*Borago officinalis.*	March or April.	Has gallant blue flowers. Good in claret cup.
Camomile (rock).	*Anthemis cupaniana.*	March or April, or in the autumn.	Casts its own seeds freely. The young plants are best, so it is wise to treat it as an annual.
Caraway.	*Carum carvi.*	The same as Anise.	Grown for its seeds. Used in cakes and comfits.
Chervil.	*Scandix cerefolium* (*Chærophyllum sativum*).	Successive sowings from spring to autumn.	An excellent pot-herb, too seldom seen in England. Useful as garnish and for flavouring.
Coriander.	*Coriandrum sativum.*	Same as Anise.	The seeds are useful in cooking and confectionery.
Cumin.	*Cuminum Cyminum.*	,,	Very rarely grown in England. Seeds strongly aromatic. Used in veterinary preparations.

HERBS GROWN FROM SEED—*continued.*

POPULAR NAME.	BOTANICAL NAME.	TIME TO PLANT.	REMARKS
Dill.	*Anethum graveolens.*	March or April.	Grown for its soothing seeds. Dill-water is still in favour in the nursery.
Marigold (pot).	*Calendula officinalis.*	Any time.	Once in the garden, will seed itself. Petals used in many herbal simples and in cooking.
Marjoram (sweet).	*Origanum Marjorana.*	March or April, or raised in heat, if preferred.	A delightful kitchen herb. Good both in parlour and garden.
Parsley.	*Petroselinum sativum.*	Sow at intervals all the year round.	Needs no recommendation.
Purslanes.	*Portulaca oleracea* and *sativa.*	March or April, or raised in heat, if preferred.	Useful for pickling or in salad.
Rampion.	*Campanula rapunculus.*	April.	A useful winter salad ; both leaves and roots are eaten.
Rock Camomile.	*Anthemis cupaniana.*	See Camomile (rock).	
Scurvy-grass, or Spoonwort.	*Cochlearia officinalis.*	Any time.	The leaves of English Scurvy-grass resemble the bowl of a spoon. One of the most effectual antiscorbutic plants known. May be relied on to seed itself.
Sea Tree-Mallow.	*Lavatera arborea.*	,,	Seeds itself freely, so that young plants can always be saved. Lives through mild winters. Grows into a small tree with a stout woody stem
Skirrets.	*Sium Sisarum.*	March or April.	A very old-fashioned vegetable. Seldom grown nowadays.
Summer Savory.	*Satureia hortensis.*	March or April, or raised in heat, if preferred.	This useful herb gives a pleasant flavour in soups and sauces. A less woody plant than Winter Savory.

INDEX

THE CHARM OF GARDENS

By DION CLAYTON CALTHROP

Containing 32 full-page Illustrations in Colour
Crown 4to., cloth, gilt top

Price 7s. 6d. net   (*By post,* 7/11)

" Pleasant and interesting to read, it embodies in its lightly-moving chapters much solid information, and must prove welcome to anyone who is fond of a garden."—*Scotsman.*

" The lover of gardens . . . will feel a particular gratitude towards the author of these varied and thoroughly pleasant chapters on garden lore, garden moods, and garden incidents "—*Daily Mail.*

DUTCH BULBS & GARDENS

Painted by MIMA NIXON
Described by UNA SILBERRAD and SOPHIE LYALL

Containing 24 full-page Illustrations in Colour
Square demy 8vo., cloth, gilt top

Price 7s. 6d. net   (*By post,* 7/11)

" Over the pictures in this book it is difficult not to wax enthusiastic, for they are veritable triumphs of colour printing."—*Globe.*

" Her pictures as a whole are as successful as the subject and the letterpress in helping to endow this volume with a unique charm which no flower or garden lover can fail to appreciate."—*World.*

ALPINE FLOWERS AND GARDENS

Painted and Described by G. FLEMWELL

Containing 20 full-page Illustrations in Colour
Square demy 8vo., cloth, gilt top

Price 7s. 6d. net   (*By post,* 7/11)

" The maker of this handsome volume writes with sympathy and botanical knowledge, and paints the scheme of flower-dappled steeps and crags as one inspired by beauty and truth. It is a masterly series of pictures which he presents us."—*Daily Mail.*

" We heartily commend this beautiful book."—*Guardian.*

PUBLISHED BY
ADAM AND CHARLES BLACK, 4, 5 & 6, SOHO SQUARE, LONDON, W.